Betty Crocker
DINNER PARTIES

Director of Photography: LEN WEISS

Golden Press · New York

WESTERN PUBLISHING COMPANY, INC.
RACINE, WISCONSIN

Seventh Printing, 1978

Dear Hostess:

There's something new on the party circuit. It's a free and easy spirit of spontaneous fun that makes today's entertaining merrier and more relaxed than ever. And this book spells out the ground rules for such delightful dinner parties. We've planned our menus for four types of entertaining: the casual, sometimes even spur-of-the-moment dinner; the meal that cooks at the table; the wonderfully flexible buffet; and the slightly more traditional sit-down dinner.

None of these meals takes more than an hour of immediate pre-party time to prepare (many, considerably less) and every menu includes a complete timetable to make absolutely certain that nothing is forgotten in the press of the last moment. Some of our dinners are based on cook-ahead dishes, some on convenience foods in gourmet combinations, and some on delicatessen specialties artfully augmented for a home-cooked taste.

Since everyone agrees that part of any party is its presentation, we've included scores of serving suggestions and dozens of attractive and unusual ideas for centerpieces, table decor and eye-catching arrangements of the food itself.

But perhaps most important, we've put all of the menus to the party test. First, the recipes are thoroughly tested in the Betty Crocker Kitchens by trained home economists; then we ask hostesses across the country to try them out on their own guests to make sure there are no snags, slip-ups or semi-successes, that every one is a triumph every time.

No matter how limited your experience, how crowded your days, or how small your home, there's a dinner party you can give with a flourish. Practice it once on the family (to give you confidence) and then send out the invitations. We're sure you'll have just as much fun as your guests.

Cordially,

Betty Crocker

Contents

Casual
and Impromptu
Entertaining

Casual and Impromptu Entertaining

Fun—it's the whole point in having a party. And today, that means fun for the hostess as well as the guests. Our new easygoing life-style has spawned a new kind of party: casual, friendly and relaxed, where the festivity lies in informal gaiety and there are no unbreakable rules.

It's the perfect atmosphere for catching up on news with old friends, or getting to know an acquaintance or even a stranger better. It's ideal for mixing people of different ages, and a wonderful way to entertain if your house is small and your equipment limited. The secrets are simple: an air of conviviality, a feeling of spontaneity in the food, the table setting and the service that makes everyone feel happily at home.

The menus in this chapter are carefully calculated to produce the look of ease. Some are especially intended for outdoor eating, supper on the patio or a picnic at the shore or on the tailgate of your station wagon. One is a joint effort, a progressive dinner—each hostess is responsible for just one course.

And still others are spur-of-the-moment parties, made possible because all the party wherewithal is in the freezer or on a kitchen shelf, ready and waiting. Then, when your husband brings a bachelor friend home after work or out-of-town cousins drop by for a surprise visit, you can spontaneously (and confidently) urge them to stay for dinner.

There are working wife and career girl specials, too, foods you can pick up at the delicatessen on your way home and dress up with sauces, seasonings and garnishes in a matter of minutes. These impromptu menus include market lists, so you can see at a glance what's needed (staples aren't listed).

Where do you serve dinners like these? The choice is unlimited. You can, of course, serve at the dining room table, or you can be as imaginative as you like in your choice of locale. Make a buffet of your bookcase. Light up a chafing dish on the coffee table. Set out serving dishes on the counter. Use a card table on the terrace, a picnic table in the yard or stack tables in the den. Let guests sit on plastic cubes, ottomans, footstools or even cushions on the floor. They can eat from trays, TV tables, or whatever surface is solid and convenient.

Add to the mood with a roaring fire, or background music from the stereo (keep it turned low so talk can flow freely). Play a simple memory game: "How many kinds of cars can you remember that aren't made today?" or "What was the first job you ever had?" And remember that in this sort of entertaining participation is the watchword. If anyone offers to toss the salad, pour the coffee or clear the table, let him. Some of the best parties are the ones that end up in the kitchen with everyone singing folk songs while they help with the dishes.

Deli Dinner in Disguise

Barbecued Deli Chicken
Hot Spiced Fruit 'n Melon
Onion Rolls   Garden Patch Coleslaw
Wine with Cheese and Crackers
Demitasse with Chocolate Mints

BARBECUED DELI CHICKEN

Heat oven to 325°. Split 2 ready-to-serve barbecued chickens (from delicatessen) into halves. Arrange halves skin side up on large heat-resistant platter or in ungreased baking pan, 13x9x2 inches. Brush with bottled Italian salad dressing or barbecue sauce. Heat 15 to 20 minutes.

4 servings.

HOT SPICED FRUIT 'N MELON

1 can (17 ounces) fruits for salad
1 jar (10 ounces) watermelon pickles
¼ teaspoon allspice

Combine fruits for salad (with syrup), pickles (with syrup) and allspice in saucepan; heat to boiling, stirring occasionally. Serve hot.

4 servings.

ONION ROLLS

Heat oven to 325°. Cut each of 6 onion rolls into 3 strips. Reassemble rolls; wrap in 24x18-inch piece of heavy-duty aluminum foil. Heat 10 minutes.

4 servings.

GARDEN PATCH COLESLAW

1 package (10 ounces) frozen green peas
2 tablespoons bottled Italian salad
   dressing
1 pint coleslaw (from delicatessen)

Place frozen peas in colander or sieve; run cold water over peas just until thawed, about ½ minute. Drain peas; place in bowl. Drizzle salad dressing over peas and toss until coated. Place coleslaw in serving dish, making a large indentation in center. Pour peas in center of coleslaw.

4 servings.

TIMETABLE

20 minutes before serving:
   Place chicken in oven
   Set table
   Arrange cheese tray
10 minutes before:
   Slice and wrap rolls; heat
   Prepare Hot Spiced Fruit 'n Melon
   Make Garden Patch Coleslaw

WINE WITH CHEESE AND CRACKERS

On tray, arrange an assortment of crackers with 8-ounce round of Gouda cheese and 4-ounce piece each Gourmandise and blue cheese.

Serve with a dessert wine such as sherry, port, Marsala, Madeira or Tokay or, if desired, cranberry cocktail.

4 servings.

SUBSTITUTIONS

■ Cheddar, Edam or Gruyère for Gouda cheese

■ Cream, Bel Paese or mild Brie for Gourmandise cheese

■ Roquefort or Gorgonzola for blue cheese

DEMITASSE WITH CHOCOLATE MINTS

Prepare 4 servings espresso or double-strength coffee. Serve in demitasse cups and accompany with chocolate mints. Demitasse is often served with a twist of lemon peel. Sugar may be offered but cream is usually avoided.

4 servings.

FOR YOUR PARTY

Expecting company at the end of a busy work day? The solution is simple. A stop at the delicatessen counter on the way home, a few easy artistries in your own kitchen, and dinner can be ready to serve in twenty speedy minutes. For a change of scene, have your party on a balcony, terrace or patio. Serve the dessert wine in a pretty decanter and have it ready with the cheese and crackers on a side table or serving cart. Be sure the cheese is brought to room temperature before serving. Then move to the living room for thin chocolate mints and demitasse—double-strength coffee served in small cups. Add twists of lemon, if you like.

Market List

1 can (17 oz.) fruits for salad
1 jar (10 oz.) watermelon pickles
1 bottle dessert wine
Instant espresso
Onion rolls
Crackers
4 oz. each Gourmandise and blue cheese
8-oz. round Gouda cheese
1 pkg. (10 oz.) frozen green peas
Chocolate mints
2 ready-to-serve barbecued chickens
1 pt. coleslaw

Shop on the Way Home

Crab-stuffed Ham Rolls
Buttered Rice   Lemon Asparagus
Avocado-Tomato Salad
Brioches
Cherries Jubilee
Coffee

CRAB-STUFFED HAM ROLLS

2 packages (6 ounces each) frozen
  cooked crabmeat
12 thin slices boiled ham (about ½
  pound)
  Curry Sauce (right)
  Sliced green onions or capers

Heat oven to 350°. Cut each block of frozen crabmeat crosswise into 6 sticks, each ½ inch wide. Place frozen stick of crabmeat at narrow end of each ham slice; roll up and secure with wooden pick. Place seam side down in ungreased baking pan, 13x9x2 inches. Cover; bake 20 minutes or until heated through.

While ham rolls are baking, prepare Curry Sauce. Arrange ham rolls on serving platter; spoon sauce over rolls and sprinkle with sliced green onions.

4 or 5 servings.

Note: 2 cans (7½ ounces each) crabmeat, drained and cartilage removed, can be substituted for the frozen cooked crabmeat.

CURRY SAUCE

2 tablespoons butter or margarine
2 tablespoons flour
¼ teaspoon salt
¼ teaspoon curry powder
⅛ teaspoon pepper
1 cup milk
1 teaspoon sherry or sherry flavoring

Melt butter in saucepan over low heat. Blend in flour, salt, curry powder and pepper. Cook over low heat, stirring until mixture is smooth and bubbly. Remove from heat. Stir in milk and sherry. Heat to boiling, stirring constantly. Boil and stir 1 minute.

1 cup.

TIMETABLE

45 minutes before serving:
  Set table
  Assemble ingredients for dessert
  Prepare ham rolls for baking
  Cook 2 packages (12 ounces each) frozen
    buttered rice
20 minutes before:
  Bake ham rolls and prepare sauce
  Cook asparagus
10 minutes before:
  Wrap brioches in foil; warm in oven
  Make coffee and salad

LEMON ASPARAGUS

2 packages (10 ounces each)
  frozen asparagus spears
2 tablespoons butter or margarine
  Lemon juice

In a large skillet, cook asparagus spears as directed on package. Dot with butter and sprinkle with lemon juice.

4 or 5 servings.

AVOCADO-TOMATO SALAD

1 ripe avocado
  Bottled oil-and-vinegar salad dressing
2 or 3 medium tomatoes, cut into
  wedges
  Curly endive

Peel avocado and cut into slices. Sprinkle with salad dressing. Arrange avocado slices, tomato wedges and endive on salad plates. Serve with additional salad dressing.

4 or 5 servings.

VARIATION

■ *Hearts of Palm-Tomato Salad:* Substitute 1 can (14 ounces) hearts of palm, chilled and drained, for the avocado. Cut hearts of palm lengthwise in half.

CHERRIES JUBILEE

1 quart vanilla ice cream
¾ cup currant jelly
1 can (16 ounces) pitted dark sweet
  cherries, drained
¼ cup rum
1 teaspoon grated orange peel
¼ cup brandy

Scoop ice cream into balls and place one or two in each dessert dish. Place in freezer until ready to serve.

Melt jelly in chafing dish or saucepan over direct heat. Stir in cherries, rum and orange peel. Heat to simmering, stirring constantly. Heat brandy in small saucepan; slowly pour over cherries and ignite. Serve hot over ice cream.

4 or 5 servings.

Market List

1 jar (10 oz.) currant jelly
1 can (16 oz.) pitted dark sweet cherries
  Rum and brandy
  Brioches
2 or 3 medium tomatoes
1 ripe avocado
  Green onions and curly endive
1 orange
2 pkg. (6 oz. each) frozen cooked crabmeat
2 pkg. (12 oz. each) frozen buttered rice
2 pkg. (10 oz. each) frozen asparagus spears
1 qt. vanilla ice cream
12 thin slices boiled ham

Driftwood and air fern create a casual centerpiece.

Crab-stuffed Ham Rolls, Buttered Rice and Lemon Asparagus.

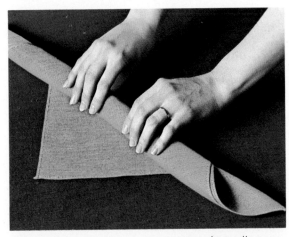

Fold each napkin once, corner to corner; then roll up.

Circle a napkin on each plate, overlapping the ends.

Cherries Jubilee—a worthy party dessert.

Progressive Dinner

> *Sherried Madrilene*
> *Crab Quiche Lorraine*
> *Great Caesar Salad*
> *Burgundy Beef*
> *French Bread*
> *Chocolate and White Fondues*
> *Coffee*

> FIRST COUPLE
> Sherried Madrilene
> Crab Quiche Lorraine

SHERRIED MADRILENE

2 cans (13 ounces each) clear madrilene
2 cans (13 ounces each) red madrilene
½ cup sherry

Heat madrilenes to boiling. Remove from heat; stir in wine and serve immediately.

8 servings (about ¾ cup each).

TIMETABLE

Night before or in the morning:
 Prepare quiche pastry and egg mixture; refrigerate

About 1 hour before serving:
 Assemble quiche and bake

10 minutes before:
 Heat madrilene

CRAB QUICHE LORRAINE

1 stick or ½ packet pie crust mix
4 eggs
2 cups light cream
2 tablespoons instant minced onion
1 teaspoon salt
⅛ teaspoon cayenne red pepper
1 can (7½ ounces) crabmeat, drained and cartilage removed
1 cup shredded Swiss or mozzarella cheese (about 4 ounces)
 Snipped parsley or parsley flakes

Prepare pastry for 9-inch One-crust Pie as directed on package except—cover pastry-lined pie pan with plastic wrap and refrigerate. Beat eggs until blended. Stir in cream, onion, salt and cayenne pepper. Cover and refrigerate.

About 1 hour before serving, heat oven to 425°. Pat crabmeat dry with paper towels. Sprinkle crabmeat and cheese in pastry-lined pie pan. Pour egg mixture over crabmeat and cheese; sprinkle with parsley. Bake 15 minutes. Reduce oven temperature to 300° and bake 30 minutes longer or until knife inserted 1 inch from edge comes out clean. Let quiche stand 10 minutes before cutting into wedges.

8 servings.

Note: Use a quiche pan if you have one—the side of the pan can be removed and the quiche served directly from the base.

SECOND COUPLE
Great Caesar Salad

THIRD COUPLE
Burgundy Beef   French Bread

GREAT CAESAR SALAD

   2 bunches romaine, washed and chilled
   1 clove garlic
   ½ cup olive oil
   1 teaspoon salt
   ½ teaspoon dry mustard
       Freshly ground pepper
1½ teaspoons Worcestershire sauce
       Coddled Egg (below)
   1 lemon
   2 cups seasoned croutons
   ½ cup grated Parmesan cheese
   1 can (2 ounces) anchovy fillets,
       drained and rolled or cut up

Tear romaine into bite-size pieces (about 18 cups). Place in large plastic bag and refrigerate.

At serving time, rub large salad bowl with cut clove of garlic. Add oil, salt, mustard, pepper and Worcestershire sauce; mix thoroughly. Add romaine; toss until leaves glisten. Break Coddled Egg onto romaine. Squeeze juice from lemon over romaine; toss until leaves are well coated. Sprinkle croutons, cheese and anchovies over salad; toss.

8 servings.

CODDLED EGG
Place cold egg in warm water. Heat to boiling enough water to completely cover egg. Transfer egg to boiling water with spoon. Remove pan from heat. Cover and let stand 30 seconds. Immediately cool egg in cold water.

TIMETABLE

Night before or in the morning:
   Prepare romaine; refrigerate
   Measure salad ingredients; refrigerate

BURGUNDY BEEF

   4 pounds round steak, 1 inch thick
   ¼ cup shortening or bacon drippings
   5 large onions, sliced
   1 pound fresh mushrooms, sliced
   3 tablespoons flour
   2 teaspoons salt
   ¼ teaspoon each marjoram, thyme and pepper
   1 cup beef bouillon
   2 cups Burgundy

Cut meat into 1-inch cubes. Melt shortening in Dutch oven; brown meat. Remove meat; set aside. Cook and stir onions and mushrooms in Dutch oven until onion is tender, adding shortening if necessary. Remove vegetables; cover and refrigerate.

In Dutch oven, sprinkle meat with flour and seasonings. Stir in bouillon and wine. Cover; simmer until meat is tender, about 1¼ hours. Liquid should just cover meat. If necessary, add more bouillon and wine (1 part bouillon to 2 parts wine). Remove from heat. Cover and refrigerate.

About 15 minutes before serving, add mushrooms and onion to meat in Dutch oven. Heat through, stirring occasionally.

8 servings.

TIMETABLE

Night before or in the morning:
   Prepare Burgundy Beef; refrigerate
   Slice French bread; wrap in foil
About 15 minutes before serving:
   Heat Burgundy Beef
   Heat bread in 350° oven

13

FOURTH COUPLE
Chocolate and White Fondues
Coffee

CHOCOLATE FONDUE

**12 ounces milk chocolate or sweet
  cooking chocolate**
¾ cup light cream
**2 tablespoons kirsch or brandy
  or, if desired, 2 teaspoons
  powdered instant coffee
  Dippers (below)**

Heat chocolate in cream over low heat, stirring until chocolate is melted. Remove from heat; stir in liqueur. Pour into fondue pot or chafing dish to keep warm. Guests select choice of Dippers and place on dessert plates; then, with long-handled forks, they dip each one into chocolate mixture.

8 servings.

DIPPERS

Fresh strawberries
Sliced bananas
Pineapple chunks
Peach chunks
Pear chunks
Mandarin orange segments
Maraschino cherries
Apple wedges
Seedless green grapes
Cubes of pound cake
Cubes of angel food cake
Marshmallows

WHITE FONDUE

Follow directions for Chocolate Fondue (above) except—substitute white almond bark coating for the milk chocolate and decrease light cream to ⅓ cup.

TIMETABLE

Night before or in the morning:
  Prepare Dippers (except bananas and apples); cover and refrigerate
  Assemble ingredients and utensils for fondues

About 10 minutes before serving:
  Prepare fondues
  Make coffee
  Cut bananas and apples; dip in lemon juice and arrange with Dippers

FOR YOUR PARTY

There's something out of the ordinary about a dinner party that changes locale with every course, splitting the menu four ways so that each hostess can put all her creative effort into one course. After a leisurely appetizer course at the first house, the party moves on to the second home. There the host (or hostess) can make a dramatic production of assembling and tossing the salad in front of the guests. The third hostess then shines, ladling the Burgundy Beef into provincial bowls and inviting the guests to dunk the hot crusty bread into the delicious broth. Finally, the fourth couple have their moment of glory when they present two fondues and a jewel-like selection of fruit and cake dippers. Of course if you want to garner all the kudos, there's no law against having the whole meal at your house, and perhaps serving the appetizer or dessert in the living room.

Crab Quiche Lorraine—served from a coffee table.

Great Caesar Salad—tossed in full view of the guests.

Burgundy Beef—with chunks of French bread on the side.

Fondues—a contrast in flavor and color.

Casual and Impromptu Entertaining

Cooking the shrimp in beer imparts a subtle flavor.

Each guest selects and peels his own shrimp at the table.

A wire greens washer holds the shrimp, and children's sand pails are colorful collectors for the discarded shells.

Key West Shrimp Boil

Shrimp Boil
Cocktail Sauce
Hot German Potato Salad
Garlic French Bread
Key Lime Pie
Iced Tea

SHRIMP BOIL

3 cans (16 ounces each) or 4 bottles
(12 ounces each) beer or
1½ quarts water
1 tablespoon salt
3 pounds fresh or frozen raw medium
shrimp (in shells)
Cocktail Sauce (below)

In large kettle, heat beer and salt to boiling. Add shrimp; heat just to boiling. Reduce heat; cover and simmer 3 to 5 minutes. Drain; serve with Cocktail Sauce. Guests peel their own shrimp. (Provide containers for the discarded shells.)

4 or 5 servings.

COCKTAIL SAUCE
½ cup catsup
2 to 3 teaspoons horseradish
2 tablespoons lemon juice

Stir together all ingredients in small bowl.

About ⅔ cup.

HOT GERMAN POTATO SALAD

4 slices bacon
1 package (5.5 ounces) scalloped potatoes
3 cups water
3 to 4 tablespoons vinegar
1 hard-cooked egg
Lettuce cups
3 or 4 small tomatoes, cut into wedges
1 green pepper, cut into rings

In large skillet, fry bacon until crisp; remove and drain. Pour off drippings, reserving 3 tablespoons. Add potato slices and seasoned sauce mix to skillet; stir in water. Heat to boiling. Reduce heat; cover and simmer 25 minutes or until potatoes are tender, stirring occasionally.

Crumble bacon and carefully stir in with vinegar, reserved bacon drippings and chopped egg white (reserve yolk for garnish).

Serve hot salad in lettuce cups or on baking shells and garnish each with sieved egg yolk, tomato wedges and green pepper rings.

4 or 5 servings.

Timesaver

Omit bacon; stir in ¼ cup imitation bacon chips and 3 tablespoons salad oil with the vinegar.

GARLIC FRENCH BREAD

1 loaf (8 ounces) French bread
¼ cup soft butter or margarine
⅛ teaspoon garlic powder

Heat oven to 350°. Cut bread into 1-inch slices. Mix butter and garlic powder; spread on slices. Reassemble loaf; wrap securely in 18x14-inch piece of heavy-duty aluminum foil. Heat 15 minutes.

12 slices.

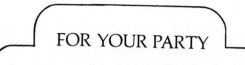

FOR YOUR PARTY

You can give your party a seaside feeling even if you're a thousand miles from salt water when you make boiled shrimp the meal's mainstay. Then echo the marine theme in simple but salty table decorations. You can even use the bright pink shrimp as the centerpiece. Place them, hot and steaming, still in their shells, in a wire greens washer ringed with rope. Set the basket on a tray to catch drips and display it against a blue or green cloth—possibly overlaid with fish netting and accessorized with sea shells, driftwood or coral. Guests shell their own shrimp, leaving the tail intact for easy dipping; they then dunk the shrimp in individual dishes of cocktail sauce. Provide children's sand pails for the shells. And present each guest with a bright terrycloth bib and offer a dampened terry washcloth or sponge for finger wiping.

KEY LIME PIE

1 stick or ½ packet pie crust mix
1 can (14 ounces) sweetened condensed milk
1 tablespoon grated lemon peel
½ teaspoon grated lime peel
¼ cup fresh lime juice
¼ cup fresh lemon juice
3 or 4 drops green food color
3 eggs, separated
¼ teaspoon cream of tartar
¼ cup shredded coconut, toasted

Prepare 9-inch Baked Pie Shell as directed on package. Cool.

In large bowl, mix condensed milk, fruit peels, juices and food color. Beat egg yolks; stir into juice mixture. Beat egg whites and cream of tartar until stiff. Fold gently into lemon-lime mixture; pile into pie shell. Chill several hours until set. Just before serving, sprinkle coconut over pie.

Note: To toast coconut, spread shredded coconut in shallow pan; toast in 350° oven until golden brown, stirring frequently.

TIMETABLE

Night before or in the morning:
  Make pie; toast coconut
  Cook egg
  Mix cocktail sauce

40 minutes before serving:
  Make potato salad
  Slice and butter bread; wrap in foil
  Make iced tea

20 minutes before:
  Heat beer for shrimp
  Heat bread
  Cook shrimp

Instant Elegance

Steak Diane
Sour Cream Mashed Potatoes
Buttered Peas and Radishes
Lettuce Wedges with Zesty Dressing
Crescent Rolls
Grasshopper Parfaits
Coffee

STEAK DIANE

2 tablespoons butter or margarine
1 pound beef tenderloin, cut into eight ¼-inch slices
¼ cup butter or margarine
2 teaspoons instant minced onion
1 teaspoon garlic salt
1 teaspoon parsley flakes
1 teaspoon lemon juice
1 teaspoon Worcestershire sauce
1 can (6 ounces) sliced mushrooms, drained

Melt 2 tablespoons butter in skillet; turning once, cook tenderloin slices over medium-high heat to medium doneness, about 2 to 4 minutes on each side.

In chafing dish at table, melt ¼ cup butter. Add remaining ingredients; heat about 2 minutes. Place meat in mushroom sauce; heat through.

4 servings.

Note: To flame sauce, heat 2 tablespoons brandy before adding meat to mushroom sauce. Pour into sauce and ignite. After flames disappear, stir sauce; add meat and heat through.

SOUR CREAM MASHED POTATOES

Heat oven to 400°. Heat 1⅓ cups water and ½ teaspoon salt to boiling. Remove from heat. Stir in 1⅓ cups instant mashed potato puffs. Stir in ½ cup dairy sour cream. Turn into ungreased 1-quart casserole. If desired, sprinkle with paprika, snipped chives or parsley flakes. Bake uncovered 10 minutes.

4 servings.

Market List

1 can (6 oz.) sliced mushrooms
Basil and poppy seed
White crème de cacao
Green crème de menthe
Instant mashed potato puffs
Chocolate wafers
Radishes
Lettuce and watercress
Dairy sour cream
1 pkg. (10 oz.) frozen green peas
1 qt. vanilla ice cream
1 lb. beef tenderloin

BUTTERED PEAS AND RADISHES

1 package (10 ounces) frozen green
  peas
½ cup thinly sliced radishes
1 tablespoon soft butter or margarine

Cook peas as directed on package. Two minutes before end of cooking time, add radish slices; continue cooking just until radishes are heated through. (Don't overcook radishes or they'll lose their crispness and color.) Drain; add butter and stir until melted.

4 servings.

LETTUCE WEDGES WITH ZESTY DRESSING

1 head lettuce, washed and chilled
4 sprigs watercress
  Poppy Seed Dressing, Curry Dressing
  or Dill Dressing (below)

Cut 4 wedges from lettuce. Place each on a salad plate; garnish with watercress. Accompany with salad dressing.

4 servings.

POPPY SEED DRESSING
Combine ½ cup bottled oil-and-vinegar salad dressing, ¼ teaspoon basil and 2 teaspoons poppy seed.

About ½ cup.

CURRY DRESSING
Combine ½ cup bottled Italian salad dressing, ¼ teaspoon curry powder and dash cayenne red pepper.

About ½ cup.

DILL DRESSING
Combine ½ cup bottled oil-and-vinegar salad dressing and ½ teaspoon dill weed.

About ½ cup.

GRASSHOPPER PARFAITS

1 quart vanilla ice cream
3 tablespoons white crème de cacao
3 tablespoons green crème de menthe
½ cup chocolate wafer crumbs (about 8
  chocolate wafers) or ½ cup chocolate
  syrup

Alternate layers of ice cream, about 2 teaspoons of each liqueur and the wafer crumbs in each of 4 parfait glasses. (Or, stir liqueurs into slightly softened ice cream.) If desired, top each with whipped cream and a maraschino cherry. Place in freezer until serving time.

4 servings.

Note: ⅓ cup crème de menthe syrup can be substituted for the liqueurs.

VARIATION
■ *White Velvet Parfaits:* Substitute orange-flavored liqueur for the green crème de menthe.

TIMETABLE

45 minutes before serving:
  Prepare parfaits
  Set table
  Cut lettuce wedges and mix dressing;
    refrigerate
  Slice radishes
  Make coffee
20 minutes before:
  Prepare and bake potatoes
  Wrap rolls in foil; heat
  Cook peas and radishes
  Cook tenderloin slices; heat mushroom
    sauce

When the Party Is a Picnic

Golden Parmesan Chicken
Green Peppers Stuffed with
Mashed Potato Salad
Vegetable Dippers with Hollandaise Sauce
Crunchy Snacks
Pecan Tarts
Iced Tea or Beer

GOLDEN PARMESAN CHICKEN

  3- pound broiler-fryer chicken, cut up
1¼ cups grated Parmesan cheese
  1 teaspoon salt
  ¼ teaspoon pepper
  ⅓ cup butter or margarine, melted

Heat oven to 425°. Grease baking pan, 13x9x2 inches. Wash chicken and pat dry. Mix cheese, salt and pepper. Dip chicken into butter, then coat with cheese mixture. Place chicken skin side down in pan. Pour any remaining butter over chicken.

Bake uncovered 30 minutes. Turn chicken; bake 20 minutes longer or until tender. Cool chicken; cover and refrigerate.

4 servings.

VARIATION
■ *Golden-crisp Chicken:* Omit Parmesan cheese and ⅓ cup butter. Melt ¼ cup butter or margarine and ¼ cup shortening in baking pan. Mix ½ cup all-purpose flour, 1 teaspoon paprika, the salt and pepper; coat chicken pieces with flour mixture. Place skin side down in baking pan and bake.

GREEN PEPPERS STUFFED WITH MASHED POTATO SALAD

  Instant mashed potato puffs
2 hard-cooked eggs, cut up
¼ cup pickle relish, drained
1 tablespoon instant minced onion
1 tablespoon chopped pimiento
2 tablespoons vinegar
4 small green peppers

Prepare potato puffs as directed on package for 4 servings. Stir in hard-cooked eggs, pickle relish, minced onion, pimiento and vinegar; chill.

Cut thin slice from stem end of each pepper; reserve slices for garnish. Remove seeds and membranes.

Just before picnic, spoon potato salad into pepper shells and top each with a reserved slice of pepper.

4 servings.

A splashy beach towel does the trick as a simple—and positively practical—picnic cloth.

VEGETABLE DIPPERS WITH HOLLANDAISE SAUCE

1 pound tender fresh asparagus or 1 can (16 ounces) vertical-pack whole green beans, drained
1 or 2 small zucchini or cucumbers
½ pint cherry tomatoes
1 package (about 1¼ ounces) hollandaise sauce mix

Break off tough ends of asparagus as far down as stalks snap easily. Wash thoroughly. Wash zucchini; remove stem and blossom ends but do not pare. Prepare hollandaise sauce as directed on package; chill sauce and vegetables.

Cut zucchini into strips. Place vegetables in plastic containers. Guests dip vegetable dippers into sauce.

4 servings.

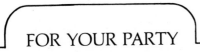

FOR YOUR PARTY

Surely there is no more casual way to entertain than with a picnic, toted to the beach or boat, or simply laid out on a brilliantly colored cloth on the porch, patio or lawn. Just be sure that the food is well chilled before it starts the trip and that it stays cold in transit with ice or cans of chemical refrigerant. And if you're leaving home grounds make a note not to forget a can opener, small salt and pepper shakers, plastic eating utensils and some packaged moist towelettes for cleanup.

PECAN TARTS

1 stick or ½ packet pie crust mix
1 egg
¼ cup sugar
⅛ teaspoon salt
2 tablespoons butter or margarine, melted
⅓ cup dark corn syrup
⅓ cup pecan halves or pieces

Heat oven to 375°. Prepare pastry for One-crust Pie as directed on package except— divide pastry into 6 equal portions. Form each into a ball and roll into 4-inch circle. Ease into muffin cup, making pleats so pastry will fit closely. (Do not prick.)

In small mixer bowl, beat egg, sugar, salt, butter and syrup thoroughly. Stir in nuts. Pour into pastry-lined muffin cups. Bake 30 to 40 minutes or until filling is set and pastry is light brown. Cool.

6 tarts.

TIMETABLE

Night before or in the morning:
  Bake chicken; refrigerate
  Bake tarts
  Prepare potato salad and green pepper shells
  Prepare vegetable dippers and sauce
20 minutes before leaving for picnic:
  Make iced tea
  Spoon potato salad into pepper shells
  Pack food and equipment

Dinner on the Double

> Deviled Ham Dip with Crackers
> Quick Turkey Divan
> Pickled Beets and Onion Rings
> Tomato-Citrus Salad
> Warm Caraway Rye Bread
> Sundae Pie à la Mode
> Coffee

DEVILED HAM DIP WITH CRACKERS

1 can (4½ ounces) deviled ham
2 tablespoons dairy sour cream or salad dressing
1 to 2 teaspoons horseradish or ½ teaspoon Worcestershire sauce
3 drops red pepper sauce, if desired
Assorted crackers

Mix deviled ham, sour cream, horseradish and pepper sauce. Serve with crackers.

4 servings.

TIMETABLE

1 hour before serving:
  Make pie
  Prepare appetizer dip; serve when guests arrive
  Set table
  Slice and butter bread; wrap in foil

30 minutes before:
  Prepare and bake turkey divan
  Make salads; refrigerate
  Heat bread
  Make coffee
  Arrange beets and onion rings in serving bowl

QUICK TURKEY DIVAN

4 slices cooked turkey* or chicken, ⅜ to ½ inch thick
1 package (10 ounces) frozen asparagus spears, separated
4 slices process American cheese
1 package (about 1¼ ounces) hollandaise sauce mix
Roasted slivered almonds
Parsley or watercress

Heat oven to 350°. Arrange turkey slices in individual shallow baking dishes or baking dish, 11½x7½x1½ inches. Place 6 or 7 asparagus spears on each slice. Cover; bake 20 minutes or until turkey is hot and asparagus is tender. Top asparagus spears with slices of cheese.

Heat in oven 5 minutes or until cheese is melted. Prepare hollandaise sauce as directed on package; pour over cheese. Sprinkle with almonds and garnish with parsley.

4 servings.

Cooked turkey can be purchased in delicatessen or can be leftover roast turkey.

PICKLED BEETS AND ONION RINGS

Lettuce
1 jar (16 ounces) pickled beets, chilled
1 small onion, thinly sliced and
    separated into rings

Line serving bowl with lettuce. Drain beets thoroughly; place in serving bowl. Arrange rings among beets.

4 servings.

TOMATO-CITRUS SALAD

Lettuce cups
1 can (16 ounces) orange and grapefruit
    sections, drained
1 medium tomato, cut into wedges
    Bottled sweet-and-sour salad dressing

Place lettuce cup on each salad plate. Arrange orange and grapefruit sections and tomato wedges in lettuce cups. Drizzle with salad dressing.

4 servings.

WARM CARAWAY RYE BREAD

Heat oven to 350°. Cut half of 1-pound loaf caraway rye bread into 1-inch slices. Spread generously with ¼ cup soft butter or margarine. Reassemble half loaf; wrap securely in 28x18-inch piece of heavy-duty aluminum foil. Heat about 20 minutes.

4 servings.

SUNDAE PIE À LA MODE

1 quart coffee ice cream
8- or 9-inch graham cracker or
    chocolate wafer pie shell*
1 pint pistachio, butter pecan or French
    vanilla ice cream
¼ cup dark crème de cacao or
    chocolate syrup

Pack coffee ice cream into pie shell. Freeze until firm, at least 1 hour. At serving time, place scoop of pistachio ice cream on each serving and drizzle with 1 or 2 tablespoons crème de cacao.

° Purchase commercially prepared pie shell or make your own ahead of time and store in freezer.

VARIATION

■ Chocolate ice cream topped with French vanilla ice cream and drizzled with crème de menthe syrup.

Market List

1 can (4½ oz.) deviled ham
1 jar (16 oz.) pickled beets
1 pkg. (about 1¼ oz.) hollandaise sauce mix
1 can (16 oz.) orange and grapefruit sections
    Dark crème de cacao
    8- or 9-inch graham cracker pie shell
    Crackers
    1-lb. loaf caraway rye bread
    Lettuce and parsley
1 small onion
1 medium tomato
    Dairy sour cream
    Sliced process American cheese
1 pkg. (10 oz.) frozen asparagus spears
1 qt. coffee ice cream
1 pt. pistachio ice cream
4 slices cooked turkey or chicken

Short-Notice Supper, Southern Style

> Quick Jambalaya
> Buttered Broccoli
> Creole Salad
> Sesame Corn Bread Squares
> Cherry Pudding Parfaits
> Coffee

QUICK JAMBALAYA

1 package (8 ounces) brown and serve
    sausage links
2 cups uncooked instant rice
2 cups water
1 can (16 ounces) stewed tomatoes
1 package (12 ounces) frozen cleaned
    raw shrimp*
2 tablespoons instant minced onion
2 teaspoons instant chicken bouillon
1 teaspoon salt
¼ teaspoon thyme
¼ teaspoon chili powder
⅛ teaspoon cayenne red pepper
½ cup frozen chopped green pepper

Cut sausages into 1-inch diagonal slices. Place in electric skillet and brown as directed on package.

Add remaining ingredients except green pepper. Heat to boiling, stirring occasionally. Reduce heat; simmer uncovered 10 minutes, stirring occasionally. Stir in green pepper; heat through. If desired, garnish with sprigs of parsley.

6 servings.

* *Rinse frozen shrimp under running water to remove ice glaze.*

CREOLE SALAD

1 ripe avocado
1 can (16 ounces) cut okra, drained
1 small onion, sliced and separated into
    rings
1 carrot, cut into thin diagonal slices
    Lettuce
    Bottled Italian salad dressing

Peel avocado and cut into slices. On each salad plate, arrange avocado slices, ⅓ cup okra, several onion rings and carrot slices on lettuce. Drizzle with salad dressing.

6 servings.

TIMETABLE

45 minutes before serving:
    Set table
    Prepare parfaits; chill
30 minutes before:
    Prepare jambalaya
    Bake corn bread
    Cook 2 packages (10 ounces each) frozen
        broccoli spears
    Make coffee
    Make salads

Create your own little corner of New Orleans anywhere—with artificial bougainvillea and wrought-iron candlesticks.

SESAME CORN BREAD SQUARES

Heat oven to 400°. Grease jelly roll pan, 15½x10½x1 inch. Prepare 1 package (14 ounces) corn muffin mix as directed except— pour batter into pan. Sprinkle with ¼ cup sesame seed. Bake 10 to 12 minutes or until golden brown. Cut into 3-inch squares.

15 squares.

CHERRY PUDDING PARFAITS

1 can (18 ounces) vanilla ready-to-serve pudding
1 cup dairy sour cream
1 can (21 ounces) cherry pie filling
Coconut

Stir together pudding and sour cream. In each parfait or sherbet dish, layer ¼ cup pudding mixture, ¼ cup pie filling, a sprinkle of coconut, ¼ cup pudding mixture; top with remaining pie filling. Garnish with coconut.

6 servings.

Market List

1 can (16 oz.) stewed tomatoes
1 can (16 oz.) cut okra
1 can (18 oz.) vanilla ready-to-serve pudding
1 can (21 oz.) cherry pie filling
  Sesame seed
  Instant rice
1 pkg. (14 oz.) corn muffin mix
  Coconut
  Lettuce
1 ripe avocado
1 small onion
1 carrot
  Dairy sour cream
1 pkg. (12 oz.) frozen cleaned raw shrimp
  Frozen chopped green pepper
1 pkg. (8 oz.) brown and serve sausage links

Serving made simple: Place the Paella and Sangría on a side table and let your guests help themselves.

Spanish Fiesta

Sangría Punch
Salted Almonds
Paella
Oranges Valenciana
Hot Cheese Bread
Caramel Flan
Coffee

SANGRÍA PUNCH

⅔ cup lemon juice
⅓ cup orange juice
¼ cup sugar
1 bottle (⅘ quart) red wine

Strain juices; add sugar, stirring until dissolved. Just before serving, combine juice mixture and wine in pitcher. Add ice; serve in punch cups. If desired, decorate cups with twists of lemon peel.

6 to 8 servings (about ½ cup each).

Note: For a mock Sangría Punch, serve Cranberry Punch (page 89).

TIMETABLE

Night before or in the morning:
 Bake flan; unmold, cover and refrigerate
 Cook chicken and combine liquid with
  tomato mixture; refrigerate
 Cook lobster; refrigerate
 Combine juices and sugar for punch; chill
1 hour before serving:
 Prepare salads; refrigerate
 Mix punch; serve when guests arrive
40 minutes before:
 Finish making Paella
 Bake cheese bread
 Make coffee

FOR YOUR PARTY

Play a lady of Spain at a party with a menu straight from that sunny peninsula. The first course consists of a refreshing red wine punch and salted almonds—a natural for serving in the living room. The delicious main course, Paella (Pah-éhl-yah) is a simple variation of a traditional Spanish dish that takes its name from the two-handled frying pan in which it is cooked and served. (If you don't have a paella pan use a large skillet for cooking, and transfer to another shallow pan or casserole for final heating and serving.) In either case arrange the food with some of the colorful seafood, chicken and pimiento on top. Put the paella pan on a side table or serving cart along with more Sangría; let guests help themselves, then take their plates to an already-set dining table.

Tip for unmolding the flans: After baking remove cups from water and chill for several hours. Just before serving run a knife around the edge of each cup, dip the bottom in hot water and unmold.

29

PAELLA

2½- to 3-pound broiler-fryer chicken, cut up
¼ cup olive oil
1 cup water
1 can (16 ounces) tomatoes
3 teaspoons instant chicken bouillon
⅛ teaspoon garlic powder
1 tablespoon plus 2 teaspoons salt
1 tablespoon paprika
½ teaspoon pepper
⅛ teaspoon cayenne red pepper
⅛ teaspoon saffron
2 packages (9 ounces each) frozen lobster tails
1½ cups uncooked regular rice
1½ pounds cleaned raw shrimp, fresh or frozen* (about 2 cups)
1 can (24 ounces) steamed clams in the shells, drained
1 package (10 ounces) frozen green peas, thawed
1 can (15 ounces) artichoke hearts, drained
1 jar (2 ounces) sliced pimiento, drained

Wash chicken and pat dry. Brown in hot oil. Add water; heat to boiling. Reduce heat; cover and simmer 20 minutes. Drain, reserving liquid. Cool chicken; cover and refrigerate. In large bowl, combine reserved liquid plus enough water to measure 3 cups, the tomatoes, bouillon and seasonings; cover and refrigerate.

Cook lobster tails as directed on package. Drain; rinse in cold water. Cut away thin undershell (which covers meat of lobster tails) with kitchen scissors. Insert fingers between shell and meat at heavy end of tail and loosen meat from shell, leaving it attached just at the tip of shell. Place lobster in bowl; cover and refrigerate.

About 40 minutes before serving, stir together rice and tomato mixture in Dutch oven or large kettle; heat to boiling, stirring once or twice. Add chicken; reduce heat. Cover and simmer 20 minutes. Carefully stir in shrimp and clams; cover and simmer 5 minutes. Add lobster tails, peas and artichoke hearts; cover and heat through, about 5 minutes. Serve in a paella pan or large shallow baking dish; garnish with pimiento slices.

6 to 8 servings.

° Rinse frozen shrimp under running water to remove ice glaze.

Timesaver

For an easy paella, omit clams and lobster tails; add 1 can (5½ ounces) lobster, drained, with the peas and artichoke hearts.

ORANGES VALENCIANA

4 or 5 medium oranges, pared and each cut into 6 slices
1 medium onion, thinly sliced and separated into rings
1 green pepper, cut into rings
Curly endive or other salad greens
½ cup bottled oil-and-vinegar salad dressing
2 tablespoons chopped ripe olives

On each salad plate, arrange orange slices, onion rings, green pepper slices and endive. Mix salad dressing and olives; spoon over each salad.

6 to 8 servings.

HOT CHEESE BREAD

1 egg
¼ cup milk
1½ cups buttermilk baking mix
1 cup shredded Cheddar cheese
 (about 4 ounces)
1 tablespoon poppy seed
2 tablespoons butter or margarine,
 melted

Heat oven to 400°. Grease a round layer pan, 8x1½ inches. Blend egg, milk and baking mix with fork to form soft dough. Stir in half the cheese.

Spread dough in pan. Sprinkle remaining cheese and the poppy seed over top. Drizzle with butter. Bake 20 to 25 minutes or until wooden pick inserted in center comes out clean. Cut into wedges and serve immediately.

6 to 8 servings.

CARAMEL FLAN

4 eggs, slightly beaten
⅓ cup caramel ice-cream sundae topping
 Dash salt
1 teaspoon rum flavoring
2½ cups milk, scalded
6 to 8 teaspoons caramel ice-cream
 sundae topping

Heat oven to 350°. Blend eggs, ⅓ cup caramel topping, the salt and flavoring; gradually stir in milk. Place 1 teaspoon caramel topping in each of 6 to 8 custard cups; pour custard over caramel topping. Place cups in baking pan, 13x9x2 inches; pour very hot water into pan to within ½ inch of tops of cups. Bake about 45 minutes or until knife inserted between center and edge comes out clean. Remove cups; chill. Unmold into dessert dishes.

6 to 8 servings.

For a dramatic finale, unmold the Caramel Flans into sherbet glasses.

31

Island Feast

> *Coconut Daiquiries*
> *Sweet-Lemon Spareribs*
> *Grilled Bananas   Island Sweet Potatoes*
> *South Seas Salad*
> *Pineapple Outriggers*
> *Iced Tea*

COCONUT DAIQUIRIES

    6 to 8 coconuts
    2 cups light rum
    2 cans (6 ounces each) frozen lemonade
        concentrate
    2¼ cups water

At the top of every coconut, there are three soft spots; pierce one of these with an ice pick or similar sharp instrument and drain liquid from coconut. Repeat with each coconut. Freeze or chill coconuts at least 3 hours.

Stir together rum, lemonade concentrate and water. Chill. Place each coconut upright in custard cup; with funnel, pour ¾ cup of the rum mixture into each coconut. Insert straw in each.

6 to 8 servings.

VARIATIONS

■ *Sparkling Orange Cocktails:* Omit rum, lemonade concentrate and water. Just before serving, stir together 1 can (12 ounces) frozen orange juice concentrate, thawed, and 1 quart ginger ale, chilled. Pour into prepared coconuts or pour over crushed ice in glasses and garnish with orange slices.

■ *Daiquiri Cocktails:* Omit coconuts; place rum mixture in refrigerator trays and freeze until slushy consistency. Serve in glasses with short straws.

SWEET-LEMON SPARERIBS

    6 pounds fresh pork spareribs, cut into
        serving pieces
    1 can (6 ounces) frozen lemonade
        concentrate, thawed
    ¾ cup bottled barbecue sauce

Place spareribs in Dutch oven. Add enough water to cover spareribs and heat to boiling. Reduce heat; cover and simmer 1½ hours or until tender. Remove spareribs to baking dish, 13½x9x2 inches. Stir together lemonade concentrate and barbecue sauce; pour over ribs. Cover and refrigerate.

Grill ribs 4 inches from medium-hot coals about 30 minutes or until glazed and heated through, turning and basting ribs often with the barbecue sauce mixture.

6 to 8 servings.

Note: If you prefer, omit grilling; heat ribs bone side down in open shallow roasting pan in 375° oven about 45 minutes, basting often with sauce mixture.

GRILLED BANANAS

Place 6 to 8 green-tipped bananas (unpeeled) on grill 4 inches from medium-hot coals. Grill 20 minutes, turning once, or until peel is black and banana is soft. Split peel; serve banana in peel with lime wedges.

Note: To cook indoors, place bananas on ungreased baking sheet; bake in 375° oven 15 minutes or until the peel is black and banana is soft.

ISLAND SWEET POTATOES

Wash 6 to 8 small sweet potatoes but do not pare. Heat enough salted water to cover potatoes (½ teaspoon salt to 1 cup water) to boiling. Add potatoes; cover and heat to boiling. Cook 30 minutes or until tender. Drain; cool and refrigerate.

Heat potatoes on grill 4 inches from medium-hot coals 20 minutes, turning often. Cut crisscross gash in each potato; squeeze gently until some potato pops up through opening. Serve with whipped honey butter.

6 to 8 servings.

Note: To cook indoors, heat potatoes on ungreased baking sheet in 375° oven 20 minutes.

Timesaver

Substitute canned for fresh sweet potatoes. Drain 2 cans (17 ounces each) sweet potatoes. Arrange potatoes on 24x18-inch piece of heavy-duty aluminum foil; wrap securely. Heat on grill 4 inches from medium-hot coals 10 minutes, turning packet frequently.

SOUTH SEAS SALAD

1¼ **pounds spinach**
¼ **cup salad oil**
½ **cup coconut chips**
  Island Dressing (below)
1 **ripe avocado**
  Lemon juice
  Salt

Wash spinach and remove stems; dry leaves. Tear into bite-size pieces (about 10 cups); place in large plastic bag and refrigerate.

Just before serving, pour oil over greens in bag; close bag and shake until leaves glisten. Add coconut chips and dressing; close bag and shake until ingredients are well coated. Pour into bowl.

Peel avocado; cut into slices. Sprinkle with lemon juice and salt. Garnish salad with avocado slices.

6 to 8 servings.

ISLAND DRESSING
2 **tablespoons red wine vinegar**
1 **teaspoon sugar**
1 **teaspoon dry mustard**
½ **teaspoon salt**
⅛ **teaspoon pepper**

Mix all ingredients thoroughly.

Casual and Impromptu Entertaining

Use an exotic flowered cloth to set the stage for your spread.

Cut along curved edge of rind with knife.

Cut pineapple crosswise into ¾-inch slices.

Pull slices to sides; fill spaces with berries.

PINEAPPLE OUTRIGGERS

2 fresh pineapples
1 pint strawberries
½ cup light corn syrup
2 tablespoons water
2 tablespoons orange-flavored liqueur
  or 1 tablespoon thawed orange juice
  concentrate

Select pineapples with fresh green leaves. Cut each pineapple lengthwise in half through green top; then cut each in half again, making 4 pieces each with part of the green top. (If serving 6, leave one half uncut; cover and refrigerate for future use.) Cut core from each pineapple quarter and cut along curved edges with grapefruit knife. Cut fruit crosswise into ¾-inch slices. Pull slices to alternating sides of shell; fill spaces with strawberries.

Stir together corn syrup, water and liqueur. Just before serving, drizzle over pineapple boats.

6 to 8 servings.

Note: Pineapple Outriggers can be completed and refrigerated 2 hours before serving.

TIMETABLE

Night before or in the morning:
  Prepare coconuts and chill rum mixture
  Precook spareribs and sweet potatoes;
    refrigerate
  Prepare spinach and mix salad dressing;
    refrigerate
  Prepare pineapples for dessert

1 hour before serving:
  Heat grill
  Finish making dessert
  Pour rum mixture into prepared coconuts;
    serve when guests arrive

30 minutes before:
  Grill spareribs
  Grill sweet potatoes and bananas
  Make iced tea
  Toss and garnish salad

FOR YOUR PARTY

This Polynesian dinner is a flexible meal that can be cooked indoors, then reheated on an outdoor grill or in the oven. Invite guests to come in costume—multicolored sports shirts for the men, muumuus for the women, thong sandals for everyone. Incidentally, a flower worn over the left ear (masculine or feminine) means "I'm looking," over the right ear "I'm taken." Appropriate decorations are practically unlimited. For example, you could spread a brilliantly patterned cloth on your table; use tiki torches, ti leaves, palms or ferns as added decorative elements—all are appropriate for this luau-like party. Use fruits and flowers, real or artificial, lavishly. If you like have leis as favors—you can buy them ready-made or make them yourself by stringing paper flowers in a big circle. Follow an island tradition and let the host put leis around the necks of women guests; the hostess can do the same for men. In each case the presentation is accompanied by a kiss. Recruit a guitar-playing friend to entertain, or play Island music on the stereo. Surprise your guests by serving the first course beverage in coconut shells. Heap spareribs, sweet potatoes and grilled bananas on one king-size wooden platter; a handsome wooden salad bowl shows off the salad nicely. Use pottery, plastic or paper plates in Gauguin colors. When the main course of the feast is finished, clear the table and serve Pineapple Outriggers on individual dessert plates.

Tailgate Party

Quick Trick Clam Chowder
or Black Bean Soup
Gourmet Beef Roast
Onion Rolls
Zucchini-Tomato Vinaigrette
Cashew Brownie Confections
Green Grapes
Spiced Coffee

QUICK TRICK CLAM CHOWDER

    1 package (5.5 ounces) scalloped potatoes
    1 can (7 to 8 ounces) minced clams, drained (reserve liquor)
    1 tablespoon shredded green onion
    1 tablespoon freeze-dried green pepper
 2½ cups milk
    1 tablespoon butter or margarine

In large saucepan, mix potato slices, seasoned sauce mix, amounts of water and milk called for on package, the clam liquor, onion and green pepper. Heat to boiling, stirring occasionally. Reduce heat; cover and simmer, stirring occasionally, about 25 minutes or until potatoes are tender. Stir in clams, 2½ cups milk and the butter; heat through.

6 servings (about 1 cup each).

BLACK BEAN SOUP

 1 can (11 ounces) condensed black bean soup
 1 can (10½ ounces) condensed beef broth (bouillon)
 1 soup can water

In saucepan, heat all ingredients just to boiling, stirring occasionally.

6 servings (about ⅔ cup each).

GOURMET BEEF ROAST

 3- pound beef rolled rump roast (high quality)
 1 tablespoon cracked pepper
 2 tablespoons shortening
 ½ cup water
 1 teaspoon instant beef bouillon
   Onion rolls

Rub roast with cracked pepper (do not rub into ends of roast). Melt shortening in Dutch oven; brown roast on all sides. Drain fat from pan; pour water over roast and add bouillon. Cover; cook in 325° oven 1 hour or until tender. Cool. Cover and refrigerate at least 8 hours. At serving time, cut roast into thin slices and serve in onion rolls.

6 generous servings.

TIMETABLE

Night before or in the morning:
 Roast the beef
 Make brownie confections
 Prepare salad

40 minutes before leaving for picnic:
 Prepare chowder
 Make coffee
 Butter rolls
 Pack food and equipment

Our versatile tailgate menu can be themed to match any occasion or season. All it takes is imagination.

ZUCCHINI-TOMATO VINAIGRETTE

3 small zucchini, cut into ¼-inch slices
3 medium tomatoes, cut into wedges
1 onion, sliced
1 can (4 ounces) sliced mushrooms,
    drained
½ cup bottled Italian salad dressing

Combine vegetables in bowl. Pour on dressing; toss. Chill at least 2 hours, tossing occasionally.

6 servings.

VARIATION

■ *Green Bean-Tomato Vinaigrette:* Substitute 1 can (16 ounces) cut green beans, drained, for the zucchini and ½ pint cherry tomatoes, cut into halves, for the tomato wedges.

CASHEW BROWNIE CONFECTIONS

1 package (15.5 ounces) fudge
    brownie mix
    Browned Butter Frosting (below)
1 square (1 ounce) unsweetened
    chocolate
1 tablespoon butter
½ cup chopped cashews

Bake Fudgy or Cake-like Brownies as directed on package. Cool.

Frost with Browned Butter Frosting. Melt chocolate and butter over low heat. When cool, spread over frosting; sprinkle with nuts. When topping is set, cut into bars, 2¼x1 inch.

36 bars.

BROWNED BUTTER FROSTING

¼ cup butter
2 cups confectioners' sugar
2 tablespoons light cream
1 teaspoon vanilla

In saucepan, heat butter over medium heat until delicate brown. Blend in sugar. Beat in light cream and vanilla until smooth and of spreading consistency.

SPICED COFFEE

6 cups water
3 tablespoons powdered instant coffee
1 teaspoon whole allspice
    Peel of 1 or 2 oranges
    Two 3-inch cinnamon sticks

Combine all ingredients except cinnamon sticks in saucepan; heat to boiling. Strain mixture and pour into thermal container; add cinnamon sticks.

6 servings.

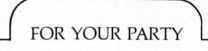

FOR YOUR PARTY

A popular way to entertain these days is a before- or after-the-game picnic using the tailgate of a station wagon as a serving table. (If you don't have a station wagon the closed trunk of your car will do just as well.) Actually, this menu is equally appropriate for a boat party, beach outing or backyard picnic. The meal has an extra fillip, especially appreciated in cool football weather—it starts out with steamy clam chowder carried in a wide-mouth thermos and poured into plastic mugs. The beef roast can be sliced at home or carved with a flourish on the scene (remember to bring a knife); the salad can be carried in and served from a colorful casserole or plastic container. Divided plates make eating easy. Keep cold foods cold in insulated containers with frozen "canned ice" or ice cubes.

Spur-of-the-Moment Supper

Turkey Ranch Rolls
Southwest Potato Salad
Three-Bean Salad
Cranberry-Orange Ice Cream
Coffee

TURKEY RANCH ROLLS

1 package (8 ounces) sliced Swiss
  cheese
2 packages (4 ounces each) sliced
  turkey luncheon meat
10 thin slices boiled ham (about ½
  pound)
2 tablespoons flour
½ teaspoon salt
¼ teaspoon pepper
¼ teaspoon allspice
1 egg
3 tablespoons shortening
½ cup dry bread crumbs
1 carton (8 ounces) horseradish dip

Cut cheese slices crosswise in half. Place slice
of turkey and cheese on each slice of ham. Roll
up, beginning at narrow end; secure with
wooden picks.

Stir together flour, salt, pepper and allspice.
Beat egg until blended. Coat meat rolls with
flour mixture. Dip each into egg, then roll in
bread crumbs.

Melt shortening in large skillet and fry meat
rolls in hot shortening, turning to brown all
sides. Meanwhile, heat horseradish dip. Place
meat rolls on warm platter and remove picks;
serve with hot horseradish dip.

10 rolls.

Note: The browned meat rolls can be kept
warm by placing in a 200° oven for 15 minutes.

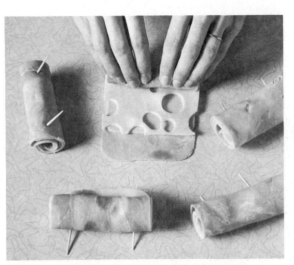

Turkey and cheese are rolled securely within ham.

Tongs are handy for dipping rolls into bread crumbs.

39

TIMETABLE

45 minutes before serving:
Blend ice cream and relish; freeze
Set table
Add ingredients to potato and bean
salads; refrigerate

20 minutes before:
Prepare Turkey Ranch Rolls
Make coffee

SOUTHWEST POTATO SALAD

1 **quart potato salad (from delicatessen)**
1 **to 2 teaspoons chili powder**
½ **cup sliced pitted ripe olives**
Lettuce cups

Stir together potato salad, chili powder and olives. Divid salad among lettuce cups. If desired, garnish with tomato wedges or parsley.

4 servings.

VARIATION

■ *Curried Potato Salad:* Omit chili powder and olives; stir in 1 to 2 teaspoons curry powder and ¾ cup salted peanuts.

THREE-BEAN SALAD

1 **quart Three-Bean Salad (from delicatessen)**
1 **jar (5⅛ ounces) cocktail onions**

Place Three-Bean Salad in serving bowl. Drain onions; carefully stir into salad. If desired, garnish with green pepper rings or radishes.

4 servings.

VARIATIONS

■ *Garbanzo Bean Toss:* Omit onions; stir in 1 can (16 ounces) garbanzo beans, drained.

■ *Mushroom-Bean Toss:* Omit onions; stir in 1 can (4 ounces) sliced mushrooms, drained.

CRANBERRY-ORANGE ICE CREAM

1 **package (10 ounces) frozen cranberry-orange relish**
1 **pint vanilla ice cream**
4 **thin orange slices**

Cut frozen relish into 1-inch cubes. Cut ice cream into chunks. Place relish and ice cream in blender container. Cover; run on lowest speed 1 minute. Stop blender occasionally and scrape sides of blender container with rubber spatula. Cover; run on highest speed about ½ minute. Divide mixture among 4 dessert dishes; freeze until firm, about 30 minutes. Garnish with orange slices.

4 servings.

Note: If you don't have a blender, thaw cranberry-orange relish. Soften ice cream; mix with relish. Freeze as directed above.

Market List

Pitted ripe olives
1 jar (5⅛ oz.) cocktail onions
1 pkg. (8 oz.) sliced Swiss cheese
1 carton (8 oz.) horseradish dip
Lettuce
1 orange
1 pkg. (10 oz.) frozen cranberry-orange relish
1 pt. vanilla ice cream
1 qt. Three-Bean Salad
1 qt. potato salad
2 pkg. (4 oz. each) turkey luncheon meat
10 thin slices boiled ham (about ½ lb.)

Midnight Supper

Sparkling Tomato Juice
Shrimp Newburg in Popovers
Crisp Vegetable Relishes
Mocha Alaska
Coffee

SPARKLING TOMATO JUICE

Mix 2 bottles (7 ounces each) carbonated lemon-lime beverage and 1 can (8 ounces) tomato sauce. Serve over ice.

4 or 5 servings (about ½ cup each).

FOR YOUR PARTY

Friday or Saturday night is an ideal time to serve a party supper late in the evening —after a movie, concert or night baseball or hockey game. And this menu can literally be on the table in minutes if the dessert and popovers are made ahead, and the vegetables washed, cut and refrigerated. While guests sip the Sparkling Tomato Juice you can finish making the Shrimp Newburg (to be served in a chafing dish), heat the popovers (be sure to have extras) and arrange cherry tomatoes, cucumber sticks, cauliflowerets, and ripe olives on a bed of chipped ice. When the main course is finished, slice and serve the spectacular Mocha Alaska in front of guests; serve with coffee.

SHRIMP NEWBURG IN POPOVERS

6 to 8 Popovers (page 42)
Newburg Sauce (below)
2 cans (4½ ounces each) medium shrimp, rinsed and drained
1 can (6 ounces) sliced mushrooms, drained
2 tablespoons chopped pimiento
2 tablespoons freeze-dried green pepper

Heat oven to 350°. Heat popovers on ungreased baking sheet about 5 minutes or until heated through. (If popovers have been frozen, heat 8 to 9 minutes.)

Prepare Newburg Sauce; stir in remaining ingredients. Cook over low heat, stirring occasionally, until heated through, about 10 minutes. Split popovers and spoon Shrimp Newburg into halves.

4 or 5 servings.

NEWBURG SAUCE

Melt ¼ cup butter or margarine in saucepan over low heat. Blend in ¼ cup all-purpose flour, ½ teaspoon salt and ⅛ teaspoon pepper. Cook over low heat, stirring until mixture is smooth and bubbly. Remove from heat. Blend 2 egg yolks, slightly beaten, and 1¾ cups milk; stir into flour mixture. Heat to boiling, stirring constantly. Boil and stir 1 minute. Stir in ¼ cup sherry.

2 cups.

TIMETABLE

24 hours before serving:
  Prepare dessert; freeze

Night before or in the morning:
  Bake Popovers
  Arrange relishes on serving tray; cover
    and refrigerate

30 minutes before:
  Prepare Shrimp Newburg
  Make coffee
  Heat Popovers
  Mix appetizers when guests arrive

Note: Remove dessert from freezer about 10 minutes before serving

POPOVERS

2 eggs
1 cup milk
1 cup all-purpose flour*
½ teaspoon salt

Heat oven to 450°. Grease 6 deep custard cups or 8 muffin cups. With rotary beater, beat eggs slightly. Add milk, flour and salt; beat just until smooth. Do not overbeat. Fill custard cups ½ full, muffin cups ¾ full. Bake 25 minutes; reduce oven temperature to 350° and bake 15 to 20 minutes longer or until golden brown. Remove popovers immediately; cut small slit in side of each to allow steam to escape. Cool.

6 to 8 popovers.

Do not use self-rising flour in this recipe.

Note: If desired, popovers can be made ahead of time and frozen.

MOCHA ALASKA

**1 package (16.5 ounces) walnut
  brownie mix**
1 pint brick vanilla ice cream
3 egg whites
¼ teaspoon cream of tartar
⅓ cup dark brown sugar (packed)
  Chocolate Mocha Sauce (below)

Bake brownies as directed on package. Cool thoroughly.

Cover baking sheet with aluminum foil. Place brownie square on baking sheet. Place ice cream on cake. Leaving 1-inch edge, trim cake around ice cream. Place in freezer while preparing meringue.

Heat oven to 500°. Beat egg whites and cream of tartar until foamy. Beat in brown sugar, 1 tablespoon at a time; continue beating until stiff and glossy. Completely cover cake and ice cream with meringue, sealing it to foil on sheet.

Bake 3 to 5 minutes or until meringue is light brown. Trim foil to edge of meringue; freeze dessert up to 24 hours. About 10 minutes before serving, remove dessert from freezer. Cut into 3 or 4 slices, then cut each slice in half. (Return leftover dessert to freezer.) Serve immediately with warm Chocolate Mocha Sauce.

Note: If desired, dessert can be frozen before baking meringue.

CHOCOLATE MOCHA SAUCE
Heat ½ cup chocolate fudge sauce and ½ teaspoon powdered instant coffee.

Cook-at-the-Table
Dinners

Cook-at-the-Table Dinners

Cook-at-the-table dinners are a delightful combination of the exotic, the sophisticated and the intimate. There's something particularly appealing about the sight of a flame flickering under a bubbling fondue pot or a handsome chafing dish. And these dinners are surefire icebreakers. Guests love the do-it-yourself aspects, the fun of cooking their own meat or dunking bread into hot, creamy cheese. And from the point of view of the hostess, there are highly practical advantages to presenting a meal that can be prepared almost entirely in advance. Not to mention the joy of a main dish that keeps the hostess out of the kitchen and free to socialize.

One kind of cook-and-eat meal is cheese fondue. This is a pot of melted cheese combined with wine. Guests swirl cubes of bread (or ham or cherry tomatoes) in the rich mixture. Though it's fun to do all the cooking at the table, it may be easier to do the preliminary cooking in the kitchen and then transfer the cheese mixture to a chafing dish or fondue pot for the final heating and serving.

Then there's beef fondue: Pieces of raw meat are cooked one at a time in a container of very hot oil, then dipped into an array of sauces and savories.

A third kind of table-cooked dinner is Oriental in origin. This offers a wide variety of combinations of meat or seafood and vegetables simmered in a seasoned broth.

Since these dinners are usually a bit foreign in flavor, they suggest all manner of appropriate table decorations. The cooking pot can often double as the centerpiece. Escargots and beef fondue can be somewhat French if the tablecloth is the traditional red-and-white check of a Montmartre café and fat red candles are in the background. Or as part of the sukiyaki setting, use a glass bowl with two or three gardenias or anemones afloat or an arrangement of small figurines.

Do keep in mind that cook-it-yourself dishes call for a little extra elbow room. Don't crowd the table. And be sure, especially with fondues, that both the pot and the dips are within easy reach of everyone. You might take the precaution of using an easily laundered or wipe-off cloth. Then if a few splatters occur, no one is embarrassed.

We've planned the dinners in this chapter for four because we believe that it's the easiest number to serve from a single cooking pot. But if you want to double the guest list, go right ahead—just use two pots.

And finally, remember that this kind of dinner is not meant to be eaten in a hurry —the self-service takes time, and the cooking itself is a major part of the evening's entertainment. So save table-cooking for extra-special times, when there's lots to talk about and you want to relax and savor every moment with your guests.

Oriental Hot Pot

> Fruit Nibblers
> Oriental Hot Pot   Dipping Sauces
> Rice
> Gingered Lemon Sherbet
> Tea

FRUIT NIBBLERS

½ cantaloupe
½ honeydew melon
  About 3 pounds watermelon
2 tablespoons orange-flavored liqueur
  or orange juice, if desired
6 to 8 small clusters seedless green
  grapes

Scoop balls from melons or cut melons into 1-inch cubes. Place 3 balls on each of 12 bamboo skewers; arrange on serving plate or tray. Sprinkle liqueur over balls. Garnish tray with grape clusters.

12 nibblers.

Timesaver

1 jar (17 ounces) fruits for salad can be substituted for the melons.

TIMETABLE

Night before or in the morning:
  Prepare dessert
  Slice meat, seafood and vegetables and
    mix sauces; refrigerate
  Cut and arrange fruit appetizers;
    refrigerate
10 minutes before serving:
  Cook rice
  Heat broth
  Make tea

FOR YOUR PARTY

Oriental Hot Pot is similar to Beef Fondue in that meat is the mainstay. However, this Eastern-style fondue includes both meat and vegetables and is cooked in chicken broth instead of hot oil, thereby cutting down considerably on the calories. Cooking and serving this dish is a delightfully lengthy affair, meant to take several hours and calculated to provide the evening's major entertainment. The classic cooking container is a charcoal-heated metal pot with a center chimney (available in gourmet departments). But you can also use an electric skillet, metal fondue pot or a chafing dish. The vital consideration is that the source of heat is great enough to keep the broth boiling. For quick cooking, the meat should be sliced very thin (easiest if it's slightly frozen when sliced). Artistically arranged food does double duty as a centerpiece. Each guest selects his own food from a platter and cooks it in his own corner of the utensil. At the end of the main course the broth still remaining in the cooking utensil can be ladled into the rice bowls and eaten like soup—the flavor is delicious.

ORIENTAL HOT POT

½ pound pork tenderloin
½ pound cleaned raw shrimp, fresh or frozen*
1 package (12 ounces) frozen scallops, thawed and cut into ¾-inch pieces
1 pound chicken breasts, boned and cut across grain into bite-size slices (¼ inch thick)
About ¼ head cauliflower, separated into flowerets and sliced
½ pound broccoli, separated into flowerets and sliced, or 1 package (10 ounces) Chinese pea pods
2 medium carrots, cut diagonally into ⅛-inch slices
½ pound fresh mushrooms, washed, trimmed and thinly sliced
1 bunch green onions (about 8), trimmed and cut into 1½-inch lengths
8 cups chicken broth**
3 cups hot cooked rice
Dipping sauces (right)

Partially freeze tenderloin; cut across the grain into ⅛-inch slices. (Or have meat retailer slice meat.) Divide meat, seafood and vegetables among serving trays or plates and arrange attractively. Garnish each with parsley if desired. Cover and refrigerate until serving time.

Pour chicken broth into 12-inch skillet until about ⅔ full (add any remaining chicken broth as needed); heat to simmer. Divide rice among 4 small bowls. Pass trays of meat, seafood and vegetables. Guests choose an assortment and, with chopsticks or fondue forks, place the food in hot broth to cook 2 to 4 minutes or until done. Serve with dipping sauces. At end of main course, guests ladle broth over remaining rice in their bowls and eat as soup.

4 servings.

*Rinse frozen shrimp under running cold water to remove ice glaze.

**4 cans (13¾ ounces each) chicken broth and 1 cup water or 3 cans (10½ ounces each) condensed chicken broth diluted as directed.

LEMON-SOY SAUCE
½ cup soy sauce
½ cup lemon juice
¼ cup sweet sake (for cooking) or sherry

Stir together all ingredients.

About 1 cup.

PLUM SAUCE
½ cup chili sauce
½ cup plum jam or grape jelly
½ teaspoon hot sauce

Stir together all ingredients.

About 1 cup.

GINGERED LEMON SHERBET

Slightly soften 1 pint lemon sherbet; stir in ¼ cup finely chopped crystallized ginger. Divide sherbet among dessert dishes; freeze until firm, about 2 hours.

4 servings.

TIMESAVER

Heat ½ cup ginger marmalade until melted. Spoon over scoops of lemon sherbet or vanilla ice cream.

Instant Orient—lacquer trays, chopsticks and *sake* cups from a novelty store. Use terry cloths for *oshibori* towels.

Bubbling Beef Fondue

Escargots
Beef Fondue
Tossed Green Salad
French Rolls
Minted Angel Cake
Coffee

TIMETABLE

Night before or in the morning:
Prepare Minted Angel Cake
Prepare Escargots for baking; refrigerate
Cut up meat and mix fondue sauces
Prepare salad greens

15 minutes before serving:
Arrange meat on plates
Wrap rolls in foil; heat
Bake Escargots
Heat oil for fondue
Make coffee
Toss salad

Escargots—a very Continental first course. For aficionados, snail plates and holders are worthwhile investments.

ESCARGOTS (SNAILS)

⅔ cup soft butter or margarine
½ teaspoon dried shredded green onion
¼ teaspoon garlic powder
1 teaspoon parsley flakes
½ teaspoon salt
⅛ teaspoon pepper
1 package (24) snail shells
1 can (4½ ounces) natural snails, drained and rinsed

Heat oven to 400°. Mix butter, onion, garlic powder, parsley flakes, salt and pepper. Spoon about ½ teaspoon butter mixture into each snail shell; insert snail and top with ½ teaspoon butter mixture.

Place filled snail shells open end up in baking dish, 8x8x2 inches. Bake 10 minutes or until bubbly. Serve hot and, if desired, with hot French rolls.

4 servings.

Note: Canned snails and the shells are available in specialty food sections. Serve them in snail plates as the first course at the dining table. Guests secure shells with snail holders and remove the meat with special forks. Any leftover garlic butter in the snail shells is delicious poured on the French rolls.

If you don't have snail plates and forks, you can serve snails on salad plates with small cocktail forks.

BEEF FONDUE

Trim fat from 2 pounds beef tenderloin, boneless top loin or sirloin steak and cut meat into bite-size pieces (¾- to 1-inch cubes). Cover meat and refrigerate. Prepare sauces at right; cover and refrigerate.

About 15 minutes before dinner, arrange meat pieces on 2 lettuce-lined serving plates. Pour salad oil (¼ melted butter or margarine may be used) into metal fondue pot to a depth of 1½ to 2 inches. Heat oil on top of range to 375° or until 1-inch bread cube browns in 1 minute. Place fondue pot on stand and ignite denatured alcohol burner or canned cooking fuel.

Guests spear cubes of meat with long-handled forks. They then dip meat into hot oil and cook until crusty on outside, juicy and rare inside. Cooked meat is transferred to a dinner fork and dipped into a sauce.

4 servings.

BLUE CHEESE SAUCE
½ **cup soft butter**
2 **tablespoons crumbled blue cheese**
2 **teaspoons prepared mustard**
⅛ **teaspoon garlic powder**

Mix all ingredients; cover and refrigerate.

About ½ cup.

MOCK BÉARNAISE SAUCE
½ **cup dairy sour cream**
½ **cup mayonnaise or salad dressing**
2 **tablespoons tarragon vinegar**
1 **teaspoon tarragon leaves**
½ **teaspoon dried shredded green onion**
½ **teaspoon salt**

Mix all ingredients; cover and refrigerate.

About 1 cup.

Note: Barbecue sauce, chili sauce, horseradish sauce or mustard sauce may be used. Or use Horseradish Sauce (page 51) or Zesty Tomato Sauce (page 59).

Protect your tablecloth and add a bright dash of color with shiny vinyl mats at each place setting.

TOSSED GREEN SALAD

1 head endive, washed and chilled
1 bunch romaine, washed and chilled
¼ cup bottled oil-and-vinegar salad
    dressing

Into medium plastic bag, tear greens into bite-size pieces (about 6 cups). Close bag and refrigerate. Pour in salad dressing; close bag tightly and shake until leaves glisten. Pour into salad bowl.

4 servings.

MINTED ANGEL CAKE

1 package (15 or 16 ounces) white
    angel food cake mix
2 tablespoons light cream
½ cup green crème de menthe
1½ cups chilled whipping cream
¼ cup confectioners' sugar
    Halved maraschino cherries
    Mint leaves or chocolate curls

Bake cake mix as directed on package. Cool. Remove cake from pan; place on serving plate.

Stir together light cream and crème de menthe. With narrow 5-inch skewer, punch several holes of various depths in cake; pour cream mixture into holes.

In chilled bowl, beat whipping cream and sugar until stiff. Frost cake; decorate with cherries and mint leaves. Refrigerate cake until ready to serve.

Note: If cake is to be frozen, place in freezer until frosting is set. Wrap and freeze. Fifteen minutes before serving, remove cake from freezer.

VARIATION

■ *Angel Alexander:* Substitute ½ cup white crème de cacao for the crème de menthe.

FOR YOUR PARTY

Although there are many kinds of fondue pots available, the best type for beef fondue is made of metal with an inward curve at the top. This helps to keep oil at the proper temperature and prevents it from spattering. Handle the oil with great care. We suggest heating it in the fondue pot on the range and transferring it cautiously to its stand in the middle of the table—within easy reach of all your guests. Then light the alcohol burner or canned cooking fuel and adjust the heat to keep the fat hot. If the oil cools so that meat is not cooking quickly, return it to the range and heat again.

The meat should be at room temperature and fairly dry to cut down on spattering. There are fondue plates on the market with sections for the sauces. Or use regular dinner plates and small bowls, such as lotus bowls, for the sauces. Two platters of beef make it easier for guests to reach the food. They then spear the meat on long-handled forks, dip it into the hot oil until it's cooked to their preference, then transfer it to a dinner fork and dip into one of the sauces. We recommend that you provide variety with a choice of from three to five sauces.

Fondue Olé

> Southwestern Fondue
> Mexicali Salad
> Sourdough Bread
> Mocha Brownie Torte
> Coffee

SOUTHWESTERN FONDUE

Remove gelatin from 1-pound cooked turkey roll;° cut meat into ¾-inch cubes (about 3½ cups). Cut 1 pound fully cooked boneless ham into ¾-inch cubes (about 3½ cups). Cover meat and refrigerate until serving time. Prepare sauces below and at right; cover and refrigerate.

About 15 minutes before dinner, arrange meat pieces on 2 lettuce-lined serving plates. Pour salad oil into metal fondue pot to a depth of 1½ to 2 inches. Heat oil on top of range to 375° or until 1-inch bread cube browns in 1 minute. Place fondue pot on stand and ignite denatured alcohol burner or canned cooking fuel.

Guests spear cubes of meat with long-handled forks. They then dip meat into hot oil and cook just until hot and light brown. Cooked meat is transferred to a dinner fork and dipped into a sauce.

4 servings.

° *Available in the delicatessen section of your supermarket or leftover cooked turkey can be used.*

GUACAMOLE SAUCE

Blend 1 can (7¾ ounces) frozen avocado dip (guacamole), thawed, ¼ teaspoon cumin and 4 drops red pepper sauce. Cover and refrigerate.

About ¾ cup.

HORSERADISH SAUCE

Mix 1 cup mayonnaise or dairy sour cream, 2 tablespoons horseradish and 2 teaspoons dried shredded green onion. Cover and refrigerate.

About 1 cup.

CRANBERRY-ORANGE SAUCE

Stir together 1 cup cranberry-orange relish and ¼ cup orange-flavored liqueur or orange juice. Cover and refrigerate.

About 1 cup.

Note: Barbecue sauce, chili sauce, horseradish sauce, hot catsup, mustard sauce or other commercially prepared sauces can be used. Or use Blue Cheese Sauce (page 49), Mock Béarnaise Sauce (page 49) or Zesty Tomato Sauce (page 59).

TIMETABLE

Night before or in the morning:
 Combine salad ingredients; refrigerate
 Cut up meat and mix fondue sauces
 Make torte; refrigerate
 Slice and butter bread; wrap in foil
15 minutes before serving:
 Arrange meat on plates
 Heat bread
 Heat oil for fondue
 Make coffee
 Spoon salad into lettuce cups

MEXICALI SALAD

1 can (7 ounces) vacuum-pack whole kernel corn or whole kernel corn with sweet pepper, drained
1 can (8 ounces) red kidney beans, drained
1 jar (2½ ounces) sliced mushrooms, drained
1 cup diced celery
½ cup bottled Italian salad dressing
¼ teaspoon salt
¼ teaspoon chili powder
¼ teaspoon cumin
Lettuce cups

Mix corn, beans, mushrooms, celery, salad dressing and seasonings in bowl. Cover and refrigerate. Just before serving, use slotted spoon to divide salad among lettuce cups.

4 servings.

FOR YOUR PARTY

No matter where you live, you can capture the colorful, informal spirit of the southwest with a party that borrows its menu and atmosphere from Rio Grande country. Which means a bit of Mexico, a hint of Texas and a sampling of the best of chuck-wagon cooking. The mainstay of the meal is our Southwestern Fondue—cubes of ham and turkey roll delicately browned in hot oil (it's a great way to use leftover ham and turkey). Make the whole affair more festive by setting the fondue pot on a tray or lazy Susan decorated with little cactus plants and filled with polished stones or sand. Use gold or rust burlap as a tablecloth and small bandannas as napkins.

SOURDOUGH BREAD

Heat oven to 350°. Cut 1 loaf (1 pound) sourdough bread diagonally into 1-inch slices, being careful not to cut completely through bottom crust.

Spread butter on slices. Wrap loaf securely in 28x18-inch piece of heavy-duty aluminum foil. Heat 15 to 20 minutes.

4 servings.

MOCHA BROWNIE TORTE

1 package (15.5 ounces) fudge brownie mix
¼ cup water
2 eggs
½ cup chopped nuts
1 carton (9 ounces) frozen whipped dessert topping, thawed
1 tablespoon powdered instant coffee
Shaved chocolate

Heat oven to 350°. Grease 2 round layer pans, 9x1½ inches. Blend brownie mix (dry), water and eggs. Stir in nuts. Spread in pans. Bake 20 minutes. Cool 5 minutes in pans; turn onto wire racks to cool thoroughly.

Mix dessert topping and instant coffee. Fill layers with 2 cups of the dessert topping mixture. Frost top of torte with remaining topping mixture; sprinkle with chocolate. Chill at least 1 hour before serving. Any leftover torte can be frozen for later use.

A decorative and practical serving idea: Center the fondue pot on a tray of small stones—the stones catch and absorb any drips. The little cacti double as favors for your guests.

Cook-at-the-Table Dinners

Salute Switzerland with these easy-to-make napkin rings. They're cut out of cardboard tubing and sprayed white.

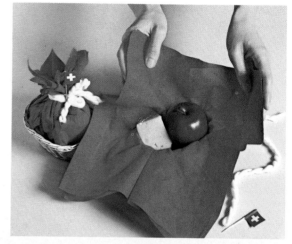

A take-home memento for each guest: An apple and cheese, wrapped in a napkin and tucked into a little basket.

A shiny vinyl cloth makes a bright and serviceable table covering for any fondue party.

Swiss Swirl
Fondue

> *Deviled Ham Appetizer Tray*
> *Cheese Fondue*
> *Tossed Greens*
> *Ice-cream Date Pie*
> *Coffee*

DEVILED HAM APPETIZER TRAY

1 can (4½ ounces) deviled ham
2 tablespoons dairy sour cream or salad
  dressing
1 to 2 teaspoons horseradish or
  ½ teaspoon Worcestershire sauce
3 drops red pepper sauce, if desired
  Assorted crackers
  Celery sticks
  Red apple, cut into wedges

Mix deviled ham, sour cream, horseradish and pepper sauce. Serve in small bowl on tray with crackers, celery sticks and apple wedges.

4 servings.

TIMETABLE

Night before or in the morning:
  Prepare pie
  Prepare appetizer spread and celery sticks;
    refrigerate
  Cut cheese into cubes; refrigerate
  Prepare salad greens
  Cut rolls into cubes; cover
45 minutes before serving:
  Arrange appetizer tray; serve when guests
    arrive
10 minutes before:
  Prepare Cheese Fondue
  Make coffee
  Toss salad
Note: Remove dessert from freezer about 15 minutes before serving

CHEESE FONDUE

1 loaf French bread or 6 to 8 hard rolls
1 pound Swiss cheese*
2 tablespoons flour
1 clove garlic
1 cup dry white wine (Rhine, Riesling,
  Chablis, Neuchâtel)
2 tablespoons kirsch or sherry
1 teaspoon salt
⅛ teaspoon nutmeg
  Dash white pepper

Cut bread into 1-inch cubes. Cut cheese into ¼-inch cubes (about 4 cups). Sprinkle flour over cheese and toss until cheese is coated.

Rub cut clove of garlic on bottom and side of ceramic fondue pot, heavy saucepan or chafing dish. Add wine; heat over medium heat just until bubbles rise to surface (do not allow wine to boil). Gradually stir in cheese, adding only ½ cup at a time and stirring after each addition until cheese is melted and blended. (Do not allow mixture to become too hot.)

Stir in liqueur and seasonings. If fondue has been prepared on range, transfer fondue pot to source of heat at table and adjust heat to keep fondue *just* bubbling. Guests spear cubes of bread with long-handled forks and dip into cheese mixture. Stir fondue occasionally. (If fondue becomes too thick, stir in about ½ cup warm white wine.)

4 servings.

*Use half Swiss and half Gruyère cheese if desired.

55

TOSSED GREENS

5 ounces spinach
½ head lettuce, washed and chilled
5 radishes
¼ cup bottled Italian salad dressing

Wash spinach and remove stems; dry leaves. Tear greens into bite-size pieces (about 6 cups). Place in medium plastic bag; close bag and refrigerate.

Turn greens into salad bowl; slice radishes into bowl. Pour salad dressing over vegetables and toss to mix.

4 servings.

ICE-CREAM DATE PIE

¼ cup soft butter or margarine
1 package (14 ounces) date bar mix
½ cup hot water
1 quart pistachio, butter pecan or
  coffee ice cream

Heat oven to 400°. With fork, mix butter and crumbly mix from date bar mix. Spread in ungreased baking pan, 13x9x2 inches. Bake 10 minutes. *Do not overbake.* Crumble baked mixture with fork. Reserve ½ cup hot crumbled mixture; press remainder on bottom and side of 9-inch pie pan. Cool.

Stir water into date filling. Cool. Soften ice cream slightly; spoon into pie shell. Spread date filling over ice cream. Sprinkle reserved crumbled mixture over top. Freeze until firm, about 6 hours. Fifteen minutes before serving, remove pie from freezer.

FOR YOUR PARTY

Cheese Fondue may have originated in Switzerland as a matter of necessity. The main ingredients—cheese and bread—are national staples, and the dish provides a good way to use slightly dry bread. But necessity or not, it's delicious, appropriate for informal dinners, midnight suppers or skiing or skating parties. Although the whole operation can take place at the table, many people prefer to melt the cheese mixture on the kitchen range, then bring it to the table where it can be kept hot for guests to swirl bread in it. Whichever way you elect to melt the cheese be sure to use a flameproof container of ceramic or heavy metal and keep the heat low to prevent stringiness. Tradition says that if a lady drops her bread in the fondue pot, she must kiss each of the men at the table; in the case of a man, he must buy the wine. The same white wine used in cooking the fondue can be served with it. Or you may prefer chilled apple juice, tea or coffee as the beverage. To add variety and color you have a choice of breads —French bread, whole wheat and rye. Or you can branch out into a choice of dippers such as halved cherry tomatoes, cubes of cooked ham, cooked shrimp, cooked small potatoes or raw slices of zucchini. With cheese fondue, long-handled forks are not essential—regular dinner forks may be used.

Sukiyaki Dinner

> Sukiyaki
> Rice
> Cucumber-Shrimp Salad
> Oriental Pear Half-Moons
> Tea

SUKIYAKI

1½- to 2-pound beef tenderloin or
    boneless beef sirloin
2 tablespoons salad oil
2 medium carrots, cut diagonally into
    ⅛-inch slices
½ pound fresh mushrooms, washed,
    trimmed and thinly sliced
1 bunch green onions (about 8), cut
    into ⅛-inch pieces
2 large onions, thinly sliced
3 stalks celery, cut diagonally into
    ¼-inch slices
1 can (5 ounces) bamboo shoots,
    drained
1 teaspoon instant beef bouillon
½ cup hot water
2 tablespoons sugar
⅓ cup soy sauce
6 cups washed and trimmed spinach
3 to 4 cups hot cooked rice

Cut tenderloin across the grain into ¼-inch slices, then into 2-inch strips. In large skillet, brown meat in hot oil. Push meat to one side. Place carrots, mushrooms, onions, celery and bamboo shoots in separate areas in skillet.

Dissolve bouillon in water; stir in sugar and soy sauce and pour into skillet. Simmer uncovered 10 minutes, turning vegetables carefully. Push vegetables and meat away from center of pan; add spinach and simmer 5 minutes longer, turning vegetables occasionally. Serve with hot rice and, if desired, additional soy sauce.

4 or 5 servings.

CUCUMBER-SHRIMP SALAD

2 medium cucumbers
1 cup cleaned cooked shrimp*
¼ cup vinegar
1 tablespoon sugar
½ teaspoon soy sauce
½ teaspoon salt
1 teaspoon toasted black or white
    sesame seed, if desired

Pare cucumbers; cut into ¼-inch slices. Place in bowl. Add shrimp. Mix vinegar, sugar, soy sauce and salt. Pour over shrimp and cucumber slices; toss. Cover and refrigerate.

Just before serving, add sesame seed and toss. Use slotted spoon to drain salad and transfer to serving plates.

4 or 5 servings.

* *Use ¾ pound fresh or frozen raw shrimp (in shells), 1 package (7 ounces) frozen peeled shrimp or 1 can (4½ or 5 ounces) shrimp.*

Note: To toast sesame seed, heat in small skillet, stirring occasionally, just until seeds begin to pop.

Oriental characters lend an authentic touch.

TIMETABLE

Night before or in the morning:
Combine salad ingredients; refrigerate
Slice meat and vegetables; arrange on
platters; cover and refrigerate
Bake half-moons but do not frost

10 minutes before serving:
Cook rice
Add sesame seed to salad; toss
Make tea

Note: 15 minutes before dessert is to be
served, wrap half-moons in foil; heat 10 minutes in 400° oven; frost

ORIENTAL PEAR HALF-MOONS

1 stick or ½ packet pie crust mix
1 can (8½ ounces) sliced pears, drained
2 tablespoons ginger or orange
  marmalade or about 1 tablespoon
  chopped crystallized ginger
1 tablespoon soft butter or margarine
  Quick Icing (below)

Heat oven to 425°. Prepare pastry for One-
crust Pie as directed on package except—after
rolling pastry, cut into six 5-inch rounds. Place
rounds on ungreased baking sheet.

Place 2 or 3 pear slices on each round; top with
1 teaspoon marmalade and ½ teaspoon butter.
Fold over dough; seal with fork and prick top.
Bake 10 to 12 minutes or until light brown.
While warm, drizzle Quick Icing on half-
moons or, using a decorating cone, make Oriental characters with icing.

6 half-moons.

QUICK ICING
Blend ½ cup confectioners' sugar and 1 to 2
teaspoons water. If desired, tint with 1 or 2
drops red food color.

FOR YOUR PARTY

Sukiyaki is a traditional Japanese dish
which combines slices of beef with an
appetizing array of vegetables and which,
according to custom, is cooked at the table
while guests watch. Arrange the sliced
raw vegetables and meat in overlapping
rows on large platters or trays; cook in an
electric skillet or on an electric griddle.
Set each place with a rice bowl, small
plate, salad bowl and teacup. If you want
to be more authentically Oriental, substitute chopsticks for flatware and serve
on a low table with guests seated on cushions on the floor. The food itself can con-
stitute the centerpiece or a simple arrangement of branches and flowers lends
an appealing Japanese note.

Cantonese Supper Party

Shrimp Roll Appetizers
Egg Drop Soup
Lobster with Chinese Vegetables
Salty Cucumbers and Radishes
or Sweet-and-Sour Relishes
Fruited Almond Float
Tea

SHRIMP ROLL APPETIZERS

Prepare 3 packages (5 ounces each) frozen shrimp egg roll as directed on package. Cut rolls diagonally into 1-inch slices. Serve with Sweet-and-Sour Sauce, Hot Mustard Sauce or Zesty Tomato Sauce (below).

6 servings.

SWEET-AND-SOUR SAUCE
Heat ¼ cup grape or plum jelly and ¼ cup chili sauce in small saucepan, stirring constantly, until jelly is melted.

HOT MUSTARD SAUCE
If packet of Chinese-style mustard is included with shrimp egg rolls, prepare as directed; or blend 2 tablespoons dry mustard, 2 to 3 tablespoons water and 1 teaspoon soy sauce.

ZESTY TOMATO SAUCE
Stir together ½ cup catsup, 2 to 3 teaspoons horseradish and 2 tablespoons lemon juice.

EGG DROP SOUP

1 can (13¾ ounces) chicken broth
4 cups water
1½ teaspoons salt
1 egg
2 scallions or green onions, diagonally sliced

In large saucepan, heat chicken broth, water and salt to boiling. Reduce heat to simmer. In small bowl, beat egg with fork until blended. Stirring constantly with fork, slowly pour egg into broth to form shreds of egg. Divide soup among individual soup bowls; sprinkle each with scallion slices.

6 servings (about 1 cup each).

TIMETABLE

Night before or in the morning:
  Prepare lobster and vegetables; refrigerate
  Prepare relishes; refrigerate
  Make gelatin mixture for dessert; chill
  Mix sauces for appetizers
45 minutes before serving:
  Arrange relishes on serving dishes;
    refrigerate
  Arrange fruits and gelatin squares in
    serving bowl
  Bake appetizers; serve when guests arrive
10 minutes before:
  Cook rice
  Prepare Egg Drop Soup

59

Cook-at-the-Table Dinners

Crush ginger root between waxed paper to retain all of the juices.

Cut bok choy diagonally into ¼-inch slices; reserve the leafy parts.

Carefully remove the stems and strings from the fresh snow peas.

Let your guests watch you cook at a side table. A black linen cloth trimmed with ribbon makes a spectacular runner.

LOBSTER WITH CHINESE VEGETABLES

2 **pounds frozen lobster tails**
2 **thin slices fresh ginger root, pared and crushed**
2 **cloves garlic, minced**
2 **tablespoons salad oil**
3 **medium stalks bok choy (reserve leafy portion; cut remainder into ¼-inch slices)**
8 **fresh water chestnuts, pared and thinly sliced**
1 **can (5 ounces) bamboo shoots, drained**
¼ **pound fresh mushrooms, sliced**
½ **pound Chinese snow peas, stemmed and strung**
1 **can (10½ ounces) condensed chicken broth (1¼ cups)**
2 **tablespoons sherry**
2 **tablespoons cornstarch**
1 **teaspoon salt**
½ **teaspoon sugar**
2 **green onions, thinly sliced**
4 **cups hot cooked rice**

Cook lobster tails as directed on package. Drain; rinse in cold water. Cut lengthwise through membranes of tails with kitchen scissors. Remove membranes. Carefully remove meat and cut into 1-inch pieces (4 cups).

In large skillet or Dutch oven, brown ginger root and garlic in salad oil over medium heat. Add sliced bok choy, water chestnuts, bamboo shoots, mushrooms and snow peas. Cook and stir over medium-high heat 2 minutes. Stir in ¾ cup of the chicken broth. Reduce heat; cover and simmer 1 minute.

Blend remaining chicken broth, the sherry, cornstarch, salt and sugar; stir into skillet. Cook, stirring constantly, until mixture thickens and boils. Boil and stir 1 minute. Tear reserved leafy portion of bok choy into bite-size pieces; add with lobster to skillet. Cook and stir until heated through. Sprinkle green onion slices over mixture and serve with rice.

6 servings.

SUBSTITUTIONS
■ 4 cups diagonally sliced celery for bok choy
■ 1 can (5 ounces) water chestnuts, drained and thinly sliced, for fresh water chestnuts
■ 1 jar (4½ ounces) sliced mushrooms, drained, for fresh mushrooms
■ ¼ teaspoon ginger and ¼ teaspoon garlic powder for ginger root and garlic (blend with chicken broth and cornstarch)
■ 1 package (7 ounces) frozen Chinese pea pods for the Chinese snow peas (increase cornstarch to 2 tablespoons plus 1 teaspoon)
■ 1½ pounds cleaned raw shrimp°, fresh or frozen, for the lobster tails

°Rinse frozen shrimp under running water to remove ice glaze.

SALTY CUCUMBERS AND RADISHES

Cut thin slices from ends of 2 cucumbers; pare, leaving thin strips of green on each. Run tines of fork lengthwise on surface of cucumbers; rub 1 tablespoon salt on each. Cover; refrigerate at least 4 hours.

Cut thin crosswise slices about ⅔ of the way through on each of 12 radishes. Sprinkle 1 tablespoon sugar and 2 teaspoons salt over radishes. Cover; refrigerate at least 4 hours.

Just before serving, fan out slices of radishes. Cut cucumbers into ½-inch slices and arrange with radishes on serving plate.

6 servings.

FOR YOUR PARTY

This authentic Chinese dinner menu requires a good deal of preparation ahead of time, but the results are well worth the effort. Moreover, with the major part of the work done you can relax and enjoy being with your guests as they eat their appetizers. For the main dish we've chosen fresh Chinese ingredients—bok choy, fresh water chestnuts and ginger root are all available in Oriental specialty stores and at some supermarkets. But we've also suggested substitutes wherever possible.

Serve the appetizers in the living room. Later, as the guests are eating their soup at the table, the hostess can cook the *pièce de résistance* at one end of the table or on a side table. The lobster and vegetables lend themselves to an attractive arrangement on a platter; use a large electric skillet for the cooking. Serve the soup in little rice bowls; when they're empty, borrow a custom practiced by Chinese families and fill the same bowls with rice. Soy sauce may be passed at the table for those who like it with their rice. The relishes, arranged on small plates or miniature trays, add a pretty, bright note. When the main course is finished, clear the table and bring in the Fruited Almond Float. This is an easy adaptation of an authentic Chinese dessert. Do it justice by serving at the table from your prettiest glass bowl.

SWEET-AND-SOUR RELISHES

4 celery stalks, cut into 3-inch strips
2 medium carrots, cut diagonally into ⅛-inch slices
1 medium onion, cut into ¼-inch slices
1 cup vinegar
1 cup water
1 cup sugar
1 teaspoon salt

Place vegetables in bowl. Heat vinegar, water, sugar and salt to boiling, stirring occasionally. Pour hot syrup over vegetables; cover and refrigerate at least 4 hours.

6 servings.

FRUITED ALMOND FLOAT

2 envelopes unflavored gelatin
2⅔ cups cold water
1 can (14 ounces) sweetened condensed milk
1 tablespoon almond extract
1 can (20 ounces) lychees
1 can (15 ounces) seedless loquats, drained

Sprinkle gelatin over ⅔ cup of the cold water in saucepan. Stir over low heat until dissolved. Stir remaining water, the milk and almond extract into gelatin. Pour into baking pan, 9x9x2 inches. Chill until firm.

Cut gelatin into 1-inch squares or diamonds. Combine lychees (with syrup) and loquats in serving bowl. Place gelatin pieces among fruits.

6 servings.

Easy
Buffets

Easy
Buffets

A buffet party is just about the friendliest party you can give. Even the shyest person mixes without self-consciousness—the very nature of this kind of dinner party makes it so. Further advantage: A buffet is the most flexible kind of entertaining imaginable. It can be formal or informal—there's the elaborate meal served from an abundantly laden sideboard and eaten at a fully set table or tables. Or there's the deliciously simple three-dish menu arranged on a counter and eaten from a plate or tray almost anywhere. And a whole range of possibilities that fall in between.

You can invite six people or sixty (if there's a porch or terrace for them to spill onto), mixing friends and neighbors with strangers and spanning the generations if you like.

You can have dinner early or late, and use anything from silver platters and fine china to earthenware casseroles and plastic plates. (For more buffet tips, see page 120.)

The success of this easygoing style is predicated on a few rules of common sense. First, figure out just where your guests are going to eat; plan your menu accordingly. If you have chairs and tables enough to go around, your choice is almost unlimited. To make it easier for your guests, set the tables with glasses, silverware and napkins.

But if you're counting on snack-table, tray or coffee-table dining, as is more often the case, you should plan your menu with ease of eating in mind. Choose foods that don't require a knife for cutting. Avoid main dishes with thin sauces or hard-to-eat salads. And what with everything going on a single plate, keep the food simple—a great casserole, a salad, bread and a super dessert.

Where you spread the buffet is a matter of your own convenience, but don't let the lack of a dining room deter you. Push two card tables together and cover with a cloth. Use a desk or chest in the living room. Bring your backyard picnic table onto the porch. Wherever you serve, if space is limited, make your food the feature attraction for your buffet "table." Use your prettiest casseroles and platters; let a colorful relish tray act as a substitute for flowers. Show off a spectacular molded salad or a dramatic dessert like Continental Lemon Cake.

All the foods in this chapter are easy to serve and most can be eaten without the benefit of a knife. Moreover, our main dishes are such that they can be kept warm without overcooking.

Although we've planned menus for groups of six to twelve, you can double or triple the recipes for a larger crowd. Just be sure you have enough oven space, equipment for cooking and utensils for serving. At party time, serve your own plate and sit down with guests. What fun to enjoy your party as much as everyone else does!

Buffet Italiano

Antipasto Tray
Lasagne
Zucchini Toss
Garlic French Bread
Biscuit Tortoni
Coffee

ANTIPASTO TRAY

Arrange any of the following in separate sections on a large tray:

Ripe or green olives
Pickled mushrooms
Green pepper rings
Pickled beet slices
Celery sticks or green onions
Radishes or cherry tomatoes
Marinated artichoke hearts
Hot green chili peppers
Cauliflowerets

TIMETABLE

Night before or in the morning:
  Make dessert
  Prepare relishes for Antipasto Tray
  Assemble Lasagne; refrigerate
  Prepare greens and mix salad dressing
  Slice and butter bread; wrap in foil

1 hour and 15 minutes before serving:
  Bake Lasagne
  Arrange Antipasto Tray; serve when guests
    arrive (or serve with buffet meal)

15 minutes before:
  Remove Lasagne from oven
  Heat bread
  Toss salad

Note: Remove dessert from freezer about 15 minutes before serving

LASAGNE

  1 **pound ground beef**
  ½ **pound ground lean pork**
  1 **can (28 ounces) whole tomatoes**
  1 **can (12 ounces) tomato paste**
  2 **teaspoons garlic salt**
1½ **teaspoons oregano leaves**
  1 **teaspoon basil leaves**
  2 **cups creamed cottage cheese**
  ½ **cup grated Parmesan cheese**
  3 **cups shredded mozzarella cheese**
 12 **ounces lasagne noodles, cooked**
  ½ **cup grated Parmesan cheese**

Cook and stir ground beef and ground pork in large skillet until brown. Drain off fat. Add tomatoes; break up with fork. Stir in tomato paste, garlic salt, oregano leaves and basil leaves. Heat to boiling, stirring occasionally. Reduce heat; simmer uncovered 20 minutes.

Stir together cottage cheese and ½ cup Parmesan cheese. Set aside 1 cup of the meat sauce and ½ cup of the mozzarella cheese. In ungreased baking pan, 13x9x2 inches, alternate layers of ⅓ each noodles, remaining meat sauce, remaining mozzarella cheese and the cottage cheese mixture. Spread reserved meat sauce over top; sprinkle with ½ cup Parmesan cheese. Sprinkle reserved mozzarella cheese in lines across lasagne. Cover and refrigerate.

Heat oven to 350°. Bake uncovered 1 hour. Let stand 15 minutes.

8 servings.

ZUCCHINI TOSS

   Classic French Dressing (below)
1 **head lettuce, washed and chilled**
1 **bunch romaine, washed and chilled**
2 **medium zucchini, thinly sliced**
3 **green onions, sliced**

Prepare dressing; refrigerate. Tear greens into bite-size pieces (about 10 cups). Place greens in large plastic bag. Add zucchini and green onions and refrigerate.

Just before serving, pour dressing over vegetables in bag. Close bag and shake until vegetables are well coated. Pour salad into large bowl or divide among lettuce cups.

8 servings.

CLASSIC FRENCH DRESSING
   ¼ **cup tarragon or wine vinegar**
   ½ **cup olive or salad oil**
2½ **teaspoons garlic salt**
   ¼ **to ½ teaspoon freshly ground pepper**

Shake all ingredients in tightly covered jar. Refrigerate. Just before serving, shake again.

¾ cup.

FOR YOUR PARTY

For a gay Italian dinner party, arrange the colorful antipasto on a sectioned tray and either serve as an appetizer in the living room or use to add a bright touch to the buffet table. Guests help themselves to Lasagne, salad and bread and, since no knives are required, eat from trays or small tables. The Biscuit Tortoni can be served later in the living room.

GARLIC FRENCH BREAD

Heat oven to 350°. Cut 1 loaf (1 pound) French bread horizontally in half. Mix ½ cup soft butter or margarine and ¼ teaspoon garlic powder; spread mixture generously on cut sides of loaf.

Reassemble loaf; cut crosswise into 2-inch slices. Wrap loaf securely in 28x18-inch piece of heavy-duty aluminum foil. Heat 15 to 20 minutes.

24 to 28 slices.

VARIATION
■ *Herbed French Bread:* Omit garlic powder. Mix butter with 2 teaspoons lemon juice, 1 teaspoon bouquet garni and dash salt.

BISCUIT TORTONI

⅔ **cup cookie crumbs (vanilla wafers or macaroons)**
¼ **cup cut-up candied red cherries**
½ **cup chopped salted almonds**
1 **quart vanilla ice cream**
   Red and green candied cherries
8 **clusters seedless green grapes**

Line 8 muffin cups with paper baking cups. Mix cookie crumbs, cut-up cherries and almonds. Slightly soften ice cream; fold in crumb mixture. Divide ice-cream mixture among paper-lined muffin cups. Arrange red cherry half and slices of green cherry on each to resemble a flower. Freeze until firm. At serving time, place cups and clusters of seedless green grapes on tiered server.

8 servings.

Crusty Curried Chicken for 12

Tomato Bouillon
Crusty Curried Chicken
Hot Peach Halves with Chutney
Noodles Almondine
Tossed Artichoke Salad
Buttered Parker House Rolls
Rainbow Sherbet Roll
Coffee

TOMATO BOUILLON

2 cans (18 ounces each) tomato juice
 (4½ cups)
3 cans (10½ ounces each) condensed
 beef broth (bouillon)
1 tablespoon lemon juice
1 teaspoon Worcestershire sauce
1 teaspoon horseradish

Measure all ingredients into 12-cup electric percolator (with basket removed) or 2-quart saucepan. Let perk through one cycle in percolator or heat in saucepan just to boiling.

12 servings (about ⅔ cup each).

FOR YOUR PARTY

Because the chicken must be cut with a knife, this buffet does not lend itself to tray service. Set up card tables instead. Heat the bouillon in an electric coffee maker and serve in the living room. Serve the chicken, garnished with peach halves and parsley, on a large platter.

CRUSTY CURRIED CHICKEN

16 large chicken breast halves
½ cup shortening (part butter)
 2 cups buttermilk baking mix
¼ cup curry powder
 1 tablespoon salt
½ teaspoon pepper

Wash chicken breasts and pat dry. In each of 2 baking pans, 13x9x2 inches, melt ¼ cup shortening over low heat. Mix baking mix, curry powder, salt and pepper in paper or plastic bag. Shake 2 or 3 chicken pieces at a time in bag until all are thoroughly coated. Place chicken breasts in baking pans, turning to coat each with shortening. Arrange skin side up in pans; cover and refrigerate.

About 1 hour before serving, heat oven to 425° Bake chicken breasts uncovered 50 to 55 minutes or until tender.

12 servings.

HOT PEACH HALVES WITH CHUTNEY

Drain 2 cans (16 ounces each) peach halves. Place peach halves cut side up in square pan, 9x9x2 inches. Spoon ½ teaspoon chopped chutney in center of each peach half. Cover and refrigerate.

About 15 minutes before serving, melt 2 tablespoons butter or margarine in electric skillet or large skillet. Place peach halves in skillet; heat at lowest setting (or over low heat) 10 minutes or until heated through.

12 servings.

NOODLES ALMONDINE

 3 packages (6 ounces each)
    noodles almondine
¼ cup butter or margarine
 6 cups boiling water

Heat oven to 425°. In each of 2 ungreased 2-quart casseroles, place noodles and Sauce Mix from 1 package noodles almondine. Measure contents of third package and divide in half (½ package is approximately 1 cup noodles, about 3 tablespoons Sauce Mix and about 1 tablespoon Almonds). Add half the noodles and Sauce Mix to each casserole.

To each casserole, add 2 tablespoons butter and stir in 3 cups water. Cover; bake until noodles are tender, about 25 minutes. Stir just before serving; sprinkle Almonds evenly over tops of casseroles.

12 servings.

TOSSED ARTICHOKE SALAD

8 ounces spinach
1 large head lettuce, washed and chilled
2 cans (3⅞ ounces each) pitted ripe
   olives, drained
2 jars (6 ounces each) marinated
   artichoke hearts
½ cup bottled herb salad dressing

Wash spinach and remove stems; dry leaves. Tear greens into bite-size pieces (about 12 cups). Divide greens evenly between 2 large plastic bags; close bags and refrigerate.

Just before serving, add 1 can olives, 1 jar artichoke hearts (with liquid) and half the salad dressing to each bag. Close bags tightly and shake until greens are thoroughly coated. Pour salad into large bowl.

12 servings.

TIMETABLE

Night before or in the morning:
   Make sherbet roll; freeze
   Prepare chicken for baking; refrigerate
   Prepare greens for salad
   Butter rolls; wrap in foil
   Fill peaches with chutney; refrigerate
1 hour before serving:
   Place chicken in oven
   Divide noodles and sauce mix equally
      between 2 casseroles
   Heat Tomato Bouillon; serve when
      guests arrive
30 minutes before:
   Prepare and bake Noodles Almondine
   Make coffee
15 minutes before:
   Heat rolls
   Heat peaches
   Toss salad with remaining ingredients
Note: Remove dessert from freezer 15 minutes before serving

RAINBOW SHERBET ROLL

1 **package (18.5 ounces) lemon chiffon
   cake mix**
1½ **cups raspberry sherbet**
1½ **cups orange sherbet**
1½ **cups lime sherbet**

Heat oven to 350°. Prepare cake mix as directed on package except—pour half the batter into ungreased jelly roll pan, 15½x10½x1 inch, spreading batter to the corners.

Pour remaining batter into ungreased loaf pan, 9x5x3 inches. Bake jelly roll pan 20 to 25 minutes, loaf pan 45 to 50 minutes or until top springs back when lightly touched with finger.

Cool jelly roll pan 10 minutes. Loosen cake from edges of pan; invert on towel sprinkled with confectioners' sugar. Trim off stiff edges if necessary. Roll cake and towel from narrow end. Cool on wire rack. Invert loaf pan to cool. Reserve loaf cake for future use.

Unroll cake; remove towel. Beginning at narrow end, spread raspberry sherbet on ⅓ of cake, orange sherbet on next ⅓ of cake and lime sherbet on remaining cake. Roll up carefully. Place seam side down on piece of aluminum foil, 18x12 inches. Wrap securely in foil; freeze. Remove from freezer 15 minutes before serving; cut into ¾-inch slices.

12 servings.

Arrange the colorful slices of sherbet roll around a styrofoam-based sunburst of multicolored plastic straws.

Easy Buffets

A prized painting can replace a more traditional centerpiece, adding extra interest to your buffet spread.

The madrilene retains its heat in sturdy cups.

TV tables are a good idea for buffet service.

Continental Lemon Cake—show it off on a serving cart or table.

Beef Stroganoff Superb

MADRILENE

3 cans (13 ounces each) consommé madrilene
1 tablespoon lemon juice
1 lemon, cut into thin slices

Heat consommé madrilene and lemon juice just to boiling, stirring occasionally. Serve in cups or mugs with slices of lemon.

6 to 8 servings (about ¾ cup each).

FOR YOUR PARTY

Make this a truly easy-on-guests buffet by setting up places at card tables or TV tables. The Beef Stroganoff can be kept hot in an attractive casserole set on a candle warmer or a pretty chafing dish. Let guests help themselves to the main part of the meal from a sideboard; they can then carry their plates to their pre-set places. And don't overlook the possibilities of adding drama to your buffet with a handsome background that can also double as a centerpiece—perhaps an oil painting or a piece of sculpture.

BEEF STROGANOFF

2 pounds beef tenderloin
¼ cup butter or margarine
1 can (6 ounces) sliced mushrooms, drained
2 cans (10½ ounces each) condensed beef broth (bouillon)
⅓ cup instant minced onion
¼ cup catsup
1½ teaspoons garlic salt
⅓ cup all-purpose flour
8 to 10 ounces uncooked medium noodles
2 cups dairy sour cream
3 tablespoons butter or margarine

Cut meat across the grain into ¾-inch slices, then into strips 3x¼ inch. Melt ¼ cup butter in large skillet; add mushrooms and cook and stir about 5 minutes. Remove mushrooms.

In same skillet, cook meat until light brown. Reserving ⅔ cup of the broth, stir in remaining broth, the onion, catsup and garlic salt. Cover and simmer 15 minutes. Blend reserved broth and the flour; stir into meat. Add mushrooms; heat to boiling, stirring constantly. Boil and stir 1 minute. Cool; cover and refrigerate.

Cook noodles as directed on package. Heat stroganoff over low heat. Stir in sour cream; heat through. Drain noodles; toss with 3 tablespoons butter. Serve with stroganoff.

6 to 8 servings.

CHERRY TOMATO-BRUSSELS SPROUTS SALAD

2 packages (10 ounces each) frozen
   Brussels sprouts
¾ cup bottled oil-and-vinegar salad
   dressing
½ pint cherry tomatoes
6 to 8 lettuce cups

Cook Brussels sprouts as directed on package. Pour salad dressing over hot Brussels sprouts, turning each until well coated. Cool; cover and refrigerate at least 3 hours.

Cut tomatoes into halves; add to Brussels sprouts and toss. Serve in lettuce cups.

6 to 8 servings.

TIMETABLE

Night before or in the morning:
   Bake cake and prepare strawberries
   Prepare stroganoff, but do not add sour
      cream; refrigerate
   Prepare Brussels sprouts for salad
   Wrap rolls in foil

45 minutes before serving:
   Arrange strawberries around cake
   Complete salad; refrigerate
   Heat Madrilene; serve when guests arrive

20 minutes before:
   Cook noodles
   Heat stroganoff
   Cook 2 packages (9 ounces each) frozen
      French-style green beans with toasted
      almonds
   Heat rolls
   Make coffee
   Add sour cream to stroganoff; heat
      through

CONTINENTAL LEMON CAKE

1 quart strawberries
½ cup granulated sugar
1 package (18.5 ounces) lemon or
   yellow layer cake mix
   Confectioners' sugar

Wash and hull strawberries. Reserve 15 berries. Slice remaining strawberries into serving bowl; sprinkle with granulated sugar. Cover and refrigerate.

Heat oven to 350°. Grease and flour a 12-cup bundt pan or a tube pan, 10x4 inches. Prepare cake mix as directed on package except—use 2 tablespoons less water. (If using yellow cake mix, fold 2 tablespoons grated lemon peel into batter.) Pour batter into pan. Bake 45 to 55 minutes or until wooden pick inserted in center comes out clean. Cool cake in pan 10 minutes.

Invert cake onto large serving plate; dust with confectioners' sugar. Place reserved strawberries around base of cake and, if desired, add lemon leaves. Cut cake into wedges and serve with sweetened strawberries.

Timesaver

2 packages (10 ounces each) frozen strawberries, thawed, can be substituted for the fresh whole strawberries.

Tetrazzini for 12

Mulled Tomato Juice
Turkey and Ham Tetrazzini
Cranberry-Orange Mold with Green Grapes
Three-Green Salad
Onion Vienna Slices
Serve-Yourself Cake Sundaes
Coffee

MULLED TOMATO JUICE

1 can (46 ounces) tomato juice
1½ teaspoons Worcestershire sauce
½ teaspoon salt
½ teaspoon celery salt
¼ teaspoon oregano
3 drops red pepper sauce

Measure all ingredients into large saucepan. Cover and heat to boiling. Serve in small cups or mugs.

12 servings (about ½ cup each).

Note: A 12-cup automatic percolator (with basket removed) can be used. Pour ingredients into percolator and perk one cycle.

FOR YOUR PARTY

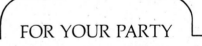

This menu gives you a chance to exercise your imagination. The salad mold might be presented on a footed cake plate; the tossed salad in a giant brandy snifter; and the frosty ice bowl filled with assorted ice-cream balls is guaranteed to be a conversation piece in itself.

TURKEY AND HAM TETRAZZINI

14 ounces elbow spaghetti (4 cups)
2 tablespoons salad oil
2 cans (10¾ ounces each) condensed cream of mushroom soup
2 cans (10¾ ounces each) condensed cream of chicken soup
1½ cups milk or 1¼ cups milk plus ¼ cup sherry
4 cups cubed cooked turkey or chicken
1 cup cubed cooked ham
½ cup chopped green pepper or dried green bell pepper
1 cup halved pitted ripe olives
1 cup grated Parmesan cheese
1 cup slivered almonds

Cook spaghetti as directed on package. Drain; pour oil over spaghetti and toss. In each of 2 ungreased 2-quart casseroles, mix 1 can mushroom soup, 1 can chicken soup and ¾ cup milk. Stir in half the turkey, ham, spaghetti, green pepper and olives. Sprinkle ½ cup cheese over each casserole. Cover and refrigerate.

Heat oven to 375°. Bake uncovered 40 minutes (30 minutes if not refrigerated), sprinkling ½ cup almonds over each casserole during last 10 minutes of baking. Garnish with ripe olives, pimiento strips or parsley.

12 servings.

73

CRANBERRY-ORANGE MOLD WITH GREEN GRAPES

    2 cups boiling water
    2 packages (3 ounces each) orange- or
      pineapple-flavored gelatin
    2 packages (10 ounces each) frozen
      cranberry-orange relish or 2 cans
      (16 ounces each) whole cranberry sauce
    1 can (13½ ounces) crushed pineapple
    ½ cup chopped celery
    12 small bunches seedless green grapes,
      washed and drained

Pour boiling water over gelatin, stirring until gelatin is dissolved. Add frozen relish, the pineapple (with syrup) and celery; stir until relish is thawed. Pour into 2-quart ring mold; chill until firm.

Unmold onto large serving plate; place bunches of grapes in center of mold and around edge.

12 servings.

THREE-GREEN SALAD

    5 ounces fresh spinach or 1 bunch leaf
      lettuce
    1 bunch romaine, washed and chilled
    1 small head curly endive or escarole,
      washed and chilled
    ¾ cup bottled oil-and-vinegar salad
      dressing
    ¼ teaspoon dry mustard
    ¼ teaspoon paprika

Wash spinach and remove stems; dry leaves. Tear spinach leaves, romaine and endive into bite-size pieces (about 18 cups). Place in large plastic bag. Close bag and refrigerate. Stir together salad dressing, mustard and paprika; cover and refrigerate.

Just before serving, pour salad dressing over greens in bag; close bag tightly and shake until leaves glisten. Pour into salad bowl. If desired, garnish with sliced radishes.

12 servings.

ONION VIENNA SLICES

Cut 1 loaf (1 pound) Vienna bread into ½-inch slices. Mix ½ cup soft butter or margarine and 2 tablespoons minced onion. Spread on slices.

Reassemble loaf; wrap securely in 28x18-inch piece of heavy-duty aluminum foil. Heat in 375° oven 15 to 20 minutes.

24 to 28 slices.

TIMETABLE

Several days before:
  Make Ice Bowl

Night before or in the morning:
  Combine ingredients for Mulled Tomato
    Juice; refrigerate
  Prepare tetrazzini for baking; refrigerate
    casseroles
  Scoop ice-cream balls; freeze
  Bake cake
  Make gelatin salad
  Prepare salad greens
  Slice and butter bread; wrap in foil
  Unmold Ice Bowl and fill with ice-cream
    balls; return to freezer
  Place Ice-cream Toppings in serving
    dishes; cover

45 minutes before serving:
  Unmold gelatin salad onto serving plate;
    garnish
  Bake casseroles
  Heat Mulled Tomato Juice; serve when
    guests arrive

10 minutes before:
  Top casseroles with almonds; return to
    oven
  Heat bread
  Make coffee
  Toss salad

SERVE-YOURSELF CAKE SUNDAES

Ice Bowl (right)
**1½ quarts ice cream (1 pint each
chocolate, coffee and dark cherry or
other flavor combinations)**
**1 package (18.5 ounces) dark chocolate
fudge or devils food cake mix
Confectioners' sugar
Ice-cream Toppings (right)**

Make Ice Bowl. Scoop ice cream into balls; place balls on tray lined with waxed paper and freeze.

Bake cake mix in oblong pan, 13x9x2 inches, as directed on package. Cool.

Just before serving, sift confectioners' sugar over cake; cut cake into squares. Place ice-cream balls in Ice Bowl and serve with cake and choice of Ice-cream Toppings.

12 servings.

ICE BOWL

Place 1½-quart metal bowl in 3½-quart metal bowl. Holding small bowl down, pour water into larger bowl until water between 2 bowls is about 1 inch wide. Fill small bowl with enough water to hold it down. Hold edges of bowl in place with 2 to 4 strips masking tape. Arrange decorative leaves or fruits in water in large bowl if desired. Freeze at least 12 hours.

To unmold, run small amount hot water into small bowl until it can be lifted out. Lower large bowl into hot water for a moment; remove bowl from ice. Place ice bowl on small plate; return to freezer until serving time.

ICE-CREAM TOPPINGS

**Maraschino cherries
Flaked coconut
Walnuts in syrup
Butterscotch, fudge, pineapple, marshmallow**

Arrange ferns on a cloth, then cover with a sheet of plastic (available in novelty stores) for a cool, shimmery setting.

For a pleasant change of pace, arrange your buffet spread for service in the round.

Greek Island Party

> Lemon Soup
> Moussaka
> Olympian Salad   Greek Bread
> Honey-Almond Tartlets
> Coffee

LEMON SOUP

1 can (10¾ ounces) condensed
   chicken broth (1¼ cups)
1 cup water
1 egg
2 tablespoons lemon juice

Measure all ingredients into small saucepan. Beat with rotary beater until blended. Heat just to boiling over low heat, stirring constantly to prevent curdling.

6 servings (about ½ cup each).

MOUSSAKA

1 medium eggplant (1½ to 2 pounds)
2 tablespoons butter or margarine
1 pound ground lamb or beef
2 tablespoons instant onion
3 cans (8 ounces each) tomato sauce
½ cup red Burgundy or beef broth
1 tablespoon parsley flakes
1½ teaspoons salt
¼ teaspoon pepper
¼ teaspoon nutmeg
   White Sauce (page 78)
1 egg
¾ cup grated Parmesan cheese
½ cup dry bread crumbs

Cut unpared eggplant crosswise into ½-inch slices. Cook slices in small amount boiling salted water 5 to 8 minutes or until tender. Drain.

In large skillet, melt butter. Add meat and onion; cook and stir until meat is brown. Stir in 1 can of the tomato sauce, the wine, parsley flakes, salt, pepper and nutmeg. Cook uncovered over medium heat about 20 minutes or until half the liquid is absorbed. While meat mixture cooks, prepare White Sauce.

Heat oven to 375°. Beat egg until blended. Stir egg, ½ cup of the cheese and ¼ cup of the bread crumbs into meat mixture; remove from heat. Grease baking dish, 11½x7½x1½, or 9x9x2 inches; sprinkle remaining bread crumbs evenly in dish.

Arrange half the eggplant slices in dish; cover with meat mixture. Sprinkle 2 tablespoons of the cheese over meat and top with remaining eggplant slices. Pour White Sauce over mixture and sprinkle remaining cheese over top. Bake uncovered 45 minutes. Allow casserole to stand 20 minutes before serving. Heat remaining cans tomato sauce. Cut Moussaka into squares; serve with tomato sauce.

6 servings.

Note: Casserole can be prepared and baked up to 24 hours in advance. Heat in 375° oven 30 minutes; it is not necessary to cool 20 minutes before serving.

WHITE SAUCE

    3 tablespoons butter or margarine
    3 tablespoons flour
    ½ teaspoon salt
    ¼ teaspoon nutmeg
    2 eggs
    1¾ cups milk
    ¼ cup grated Parmesan cheese

Melt butter in saucepan. Blend in flour, salt and nutmeg. Cook over low heat, stirring until mixture is smooth and bubbly. Remove from heat. Blend eggs and milk; stir into flour mixture. Heat to boiling, stirring constantly. Boil and stir 1 minute. Stir in cheese; heat through.

OLYMPIAN SALAD

    ½ medium head lettuce, washed and chilled
    1 small bunch romaine, washed and chilled
    8 radishes
    1 medium cucumber
    4 scallions
    ½ cup salad oil
    ⅓ cup wine vinegar
    1½ teaspoons salt
    1½ teaspoons oregano
    18 Greek or ripe green olives
    ¼ cup crumbled blue or feta cheese
       (about 1 ounce)
    1 can (2 ounces) rolled anchovies with
       capers, drained

Tear greens into bite-size pieces (about 6 cups). Place in large plastic bag. Slice radishes and unpared cucumber into bag. Cut scallions into short pieces and add to vegetables. Close bag and refrigerate. In tightly covered jar, combine oil, vinegar, salt and oregano; refrigerate.

Just before serving, shake oil-and-vinegar mixture until blended. Add olives and oil-and-vinegar mixture to vegetables in bag. Close bag tightly and shake until ingredients are well coated. Pour salad into large bowl; top with cheese and anchovies.

6 servings.

TIMETABLE

2 days before:
  Prepare dough for dessert; refrigerate
Night before or in the morning:
  Prepare and bake Moussaka; refrigerate
  Prepare salad ingredients and mix dressing
  Roll out and bake dessert shells
  Prepare cheese mixture for dessert
40 minutes before serving:
  Complete dessert
  Place Moussaka in oven
  Prepare soup; serve when guests arrive
10 minutes before:
  Place Greek breads in oven
  Make coffee
  Heat tomato sauce for Moussaka
  Complete salad

FOR YOUR PARTY

For a truly different dinner party, borrow a menu from Greece, centered around a delicious Moussaka (Moos-sah-káh). Use ground beef if you prefer, but lamb is more authentic. The Moussaka can be made a day ahead and reheated just before the party. The feta cheese used in the salad is a salty, fairly soft white cheese made from goat's milk. You can buy it, along with Greek bread and Greek coffee, in specialty food shops and in the gourmet departments of some supermarkets. If you are unable to find the Greek bread and coffee, substitute crusty rolls and strong regular coffee.

Serve dessert in the living room. A runner of gold paper lends a festive look as it protects the coffee table.

HONEY-ALMOND TARTLETS

1 cup butter
1½ cups all-purpose flour*
½ cup dairy sour cream
    Sugar Glaze (right)
1 package (8 ounces) cream cheese,
    softened
½ cup honey
¼ cup diced toasted almonds
9 fresh strawberries with hulls

Cut butter into flour with pastry blender until completely mixed. With fork, blend in sour cream. Divide dough in half; wrap each in aluminum foil or plastic wrap and refrigerate at least 8 hours (thorough chilling of the dough is important for ease in handling).

Heat oven to 350°. Roll one part pastry on well-floured cloth-covered board into a circle 1/16 inch thick. Cut into 4-inch rounds. Refrigerate scraps of dough before rerolling. In ⅔ of the rounds, cut out 2-inch circles. Place plain rounds on ungreased baking sheet. Brush with Sugar Glaze; top each with a round with center removed. Brush with glaze and top with another round with center removed (you will have 3 layers—one plain, 2 with centers removed). Brush tops with glaze. Repeat with second part of pastry. Bake about 25 minutes or until light brown. Cool.

Blend cream cheese and honey; stir in almonds. Spoon cheese mixture into tartlets. Place strawberries on tartlets.

9 tartlets.

SUGAR GLAZE
Stir together 3 tablespoons sugar and 1 tablespoon water.

Self-rising flour can be used in this recipe—but baking time may be shorter.

Stroganoff on a Shoestring

> Pow and Toasted Party Mix
> Hamburger Stroganoff with Rice
> Zucchini-Tomato Toss
> Dill Pickles
> Crusty French Bread
> Fruit Platter Pie
> Coffee

POW

4 cans (10½ ounces each) condensed beef broth (bouillon)
2 cups water
1 tablespoon horseradish
1 teaspoon dill weed

Combine all ingredients in large saucepan. Heat to simmering, stirring occasionally. Serve hot in small cups or mugs.

12 servings (about ½ cup each).

TOASTED PARTY MIX

4 cups O-shaped puffed oat cereal
1½ cups mixed nuts or peanuts
1½ cups seasoned croutons
1 cup pretzel sticks
½ cup salad oil
2 teaspoons Worcestershire sauce
½ teaspoon garlic salt
¼ teaspoon salt

Heat oven to 275°. Mix cereal, nuts, croutons and pretzel sticks in baking pan, 13x9x2 inches. Blend remaining ingredients and pour over cereal mixture; mix. Bake 45 minutes, stirring occasionally.

8 cups.

HAMBURGER STROGANOFF WITH RICE

3 pounds ground beef
3 medium onions, chopped, or ¾ cup instant minced onion
2 teaspoons garlic salt
½ teaspoon pepper
2 cans (6 ounces each) sliced mushrooms, drained
3 cans (10¾ ounces each) condensed cream of chicken soup
3 cups dairy sour cream or plain yogurt
Snipped parsley
Hot Cooked Rice (page 81)

In Dutch oven or roaster, cook and stir ground beef until brown. Drain off fat. Add onion, garlic salt, pepper and mushrooms; cook and stir about 2 minutes. Stir in soup; heat to boiling, stirring constantly. Reduce heat; simmer uncovered 10 minutes. Cool; cover and refrigerate.

About 25 minutes before serving, divide ground beef mixture between two 12-inch electric skillets (about 4½ cups mixture in each). Heat on low setting to simmering, about 15 minutes, stirring occasionally. Stir 1½ cups sour cream into mixture in each skillet; heat through. Sprinkle with snipped parsley and serve with rice.

12 servings.

HOT COOKED RICE

6 cups boiling water
3 cups uncooked regular rice
1 tablespoon salt

Heat oven to 350°. Mix ingredients thoroughly in ungreased baking dish, 13½x9x2 inches, or in 3-quart casserole. Cover dish tightly with aluminum foil or casserole lid. Bake 25 to 30 minutes or until liquid is absorbed and rice is tender.

About 9 cups.

ZUCCHINI-TOMATO TOSS

   Classic French Dressing (below)
1 large head lettuce, washed and
   chilled
1 bunch romaine, washed and chilled
2 medium zucchini
3 green onions
4 tomatoes
12 lettuce cups

Prepare dressing; refrigerate. Tear greens into bite-size pieces (about 16 cups). Place in large plastic bag. Wash zucchini; remove stem and blossom ends but do not pare. Thinly slice zucchini and green onions into bag. Close bag and refrigerate.

Just before serving, cut each tomato into 8 wedges and place in bag. Pour dressing over vegetables in bag. Close bag tightly and shake until vegetables are well coated. Arrange lettuce cups on platter. Divide salad among cups.

12 servings.

CLASSIC FRENCH DRESSING
¼ cup tarragon or wine vinegar
½ cup olive or salad oil
2½ teaspoons garlic salt
¼ to ½ teaspoon freshly ground pepper

Shake all ingredients in tightly covered jar. Refrigerate. Just before using, shake again.

CRUSTY FRENCH BREAD

Heat oven to 350°. Cut 1 loaf (1 pound) French bread into 1-inch slices. Mix ½ cup soft butter or margarine and 1 teaspoon basil leaves; spread on slices. Reassemble loaf; wrap securely in 28x18-inch piece of heavy-duty aluminum foil. Heat 15 minutes.

24 to 28 slices.

TIMETABLE

Night before or in the morning:
   Prepare stroganoff but do not add sour
      cream; refrigerate
   Prepare salad greens and mix dressing
   Combine ingredients for Pow; refrigerate
   Prepare Toasted Party Mix
   Slice and butter bread; wrap in foil
   Bake pastry shell
   Prepare strawberries and orange sauce;
      refrigerate

1 hour before serving:
   Arrange fruit in pastry shell
   Heat Pow; serve with snacks when guests
      arrive

35 minutes before:
   Bake rice
   Heat stroganoff

15 minutes before:
   Place bread in oven
   Make coffee
   Toss salad; arrange in lettuce cups
   Add sour cream to stroganoff; heat
      through

FRUIT PLATTER PIE

2 sticks or 1 packet pie crust mix
  Clear Orange Sauce (right)
1 pint fresh strawberries (reserve 6
  whole berries), washed and halved
1 can (29 ounces) peach slices, drained
  (reserve syrup)
1 medium banana or 2 cups grapes
2 tablespoons sugar

Prepare pastry for Two-crust Pie as directed on package except—roll each round into an 11-inch circle and ease into 10-inch pizza pan.

Fold under ½ inch of dough around edge; pinch or pleat edge. Prick bottom and side with fork. (If you don't have pizza pans, place circles on ungreased baking sheets and flute.) Bake 8 to 10 minutes or until golden.

Prepare Clear Orange Sauce. Arrange strawberry halves around edge of each pastry shell. Place peach slices in a circle next to strawberries. Cut banana into ⅛-inch slices and dip each into reserved peach syrup; arrange a circle of overlapping banana slices next to

peaches. Place reserved strawberries in center. Sprinkle fruits with sugar. Wrap in plastic wrap and refrigerate no longer than 4 hours.

Just before serving, spoon some of the orange sauce over fruit. Cut pies into wedges; serve with remaining sauce.

12 servings.

Note: If you prefer, substitute 1 can (20½ ounces) pineapple spears, drained, for the peaches.

CLEAR ORANGE SAUCE
1 cup sugar
¼ teaspoon salt
2 tablespoons cornstarch
1 cup orange juice
¼ cup lemon juice
¾ cup water

In small saucepan, mix sugar, salt and cornstarch. Stir in orange juice, lemon juice and water. Cook, stirring constantly, until mixture thickens and boils. Boil and stir 1 minute. Remove from heat. Cool.

Our good-for-all-seasons Fruit Platter Pie—as pretty as a picture and easy to make.

Exotic Indian Dinner

Shrimp Curry
Rice Mold   Condiments
Cucumber-Spinach Toss
Sesame Seed Wafers
Fruit Medley with Sherbet
Tea or Coffee

SHRIMP CURRY

Condiments (below)
4 cans (10¾ ounces each) condensed
  cream of shrimp soup
1 tablespoon parsley flakes
1 tablespoon plus 1 teaspoon
  curry powder
¼ cup instant minced onion
1½ pounds frozen cleaned raw shrimp*
8 cups hot cooked rice

Prepare Condiments. Combine soup, parsley flakes, curry powder and onion in saucepan; heat to boiling, stirring occasionally. Stir in shrimp; heat just to boiling. Reduce heat; cover and simmer 5 to 10 minutes or until shrimp is done.

Pack hot rice into 1½-quart mold. Immediately unmold onto hot platter. Pour Shrimp Curry into chafing dish; keep warm over low heat. Serve over rice and accompany with choice of several condiments.

8 servings.

* *Rinse frozen shrimp under running water to remove ice glaze.*

CONDIMENTS
Choose from the following: diced tomatoes, golden raisins, toasted shredded coconut, chopped hard-cooked eggs, sweet pickle sticks, chutney, chopped green peppers, crumbled crisply fried bacon, grated orange peel, grated lemon peel, salted diced almonds, currant jelly, peeled and sliced avocado, kumquats, chopped peanuts.

TIMETABLE

Night before or in the morning:
  Prepare Condiments; place in serving
    containers
  Prepare salad ingredients
  Chill fruits for dessert
  Scoop sherbet balls; freeze

45 minutes before serving:
  Prepare and arrange fruits (except
    bananas and pear) on tray; refrigerate
  Prepare curry

10 minutes before:
  Cook rice
  Complete salad
  Mold rice

Just before serving dessert:
  Slice bananas and pear and arrange on
    tray with sherbet

CUCUMBER-SPINACH TOSS

10 ounces spinach
 1 medium cucumber
½ cup bottled herb salad dressing
½ cup chopped salted peanuts

Wash spinach and remove stems; dry leaves. Tear leaves into bite-size pieces (about 10 cups). Place in plastic bag and refrigerate. Thinly slice unpared cucumber into bowl. Pour salad dressing over slices; cover and refrigerate. Just before serving, pour cucumber slices with salad dressing into bag with spinach. Add peanuts; close bag and shake.

8 servings.   83

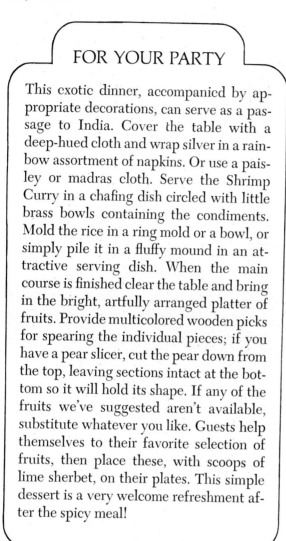

FOR YOUR PARTY

This exotic dinner, accompanied by appropriate decorations, can serve as a passage to India. Cover the table with a deep-hued cloth and wrap silver in a rainbow assortment of napkins. Or use a paisley or madras cloth. Serve the Shrimp Curry in a chafing dish circled with little brass bowls containing the condiments. Mold the rice in a ring mold or a bowl, or simply pile it in a fluffy mound in an attractive serving dish. When the main course is finished clear the table and bring in the bright, artfully arranged platter of fruits. Provide multicolored wooden picks for spearing the individual pieces; if you have a pear slicer, cut the pear down from the top, leaving sections intact at the bottom so it will hold its shape. If any of the fruits we've suggested aren't available, substitute whatever you like. Guests help themselves to their favorite selection of fruits, then place these, with scoops of lime sherbet, on their plates. This simple dessert is a very welcome refreshment after the spicy meal!

FRUIT MEDLEY WITH SHERBET

Lemon leaves or ferns
1 **can (20 ounces) sliced mangoes, drained**
1 **can (15½ ounces) pineapple chunks, drained (reserve syrup)**
¼ **honeydew melon, pared and sliced**
½ **cantaloupe, pared and sliced**
2 **large bananas**
1 **pear**
1 **quart lime sherbet**

Arrange lemon leaves on large tray, leaving space on tray for bowl of sherbet. Arrange mangoes, pineapple chunks and melon slices on tray. Place unpeeled bananas on tray; cut each banana lengthwise just through peel. Open peel slightly and diagonally slice banana. Brush slices with reserved pineapple syrup. Cut pear lengthwise into 8 sections; dip into reserved pineapple syrup and place on tray. Serve with sherbet balls.

8 servings.

VARIATION

■ *Fruit Medley with Gingered Cream:* Omit lime sherbet. Mix 1 cup dairy sour cream and 1 tablespoon brown sugar in small bowl. Sprinkle chopped crystallized ginger over top. Place on tray.

Today's
Sit-down
Dinners

Today's
Sit-down
Dinners

Who says a traditional dinner party has to be dull? Not us. Leaf through the pages that follow and see how we've updated sit-down dinners. We think you'll agree that you don't for a minute have to sacrifice graciousness in order to be contemporary.

Since very few people expect or even want an elaborate succession of courses, dinners in the new tradition have been simplified. This makes serving easier on the hostess without losing any party-time charm.

Some of the gracious amenities of the past are still fine additions to your "now" dinner party. When guests enter the dining room, you may indicate to them where you would like them to sit. Any honor guests or older people should be seated to the right of the host and hostess, and husbands and wives should not sit side by side. (Other suggestions are on page 119.)

Your guest list for this kind of dinner should be limited—eight is probably the most you can handle readily. So even if your dining table extends to seat 12, it's a good idea to give two smaller parties for six. Besides— conversation is supposed to be general, and it's easier for a small group to talk together.

If your wedding presents included beautiful china, crystal and silver, this is the time you'll want to use them. But you'll be just as "in" (maybe more so) if your table is a gay one, set with colorful pottery plates, bright plastic mugs and good-looking stainless steel. Use your ingenuity in deciding on a centerpiece. It can be a formal one of flowers, greens and candles or something gay and peasanty, depending on the food.

The food can be as elegant as our Crystal and Candlelight menu on page 115 or as hearty and provincial as the Brittany Farm Supper on page 111, with any degree of variation in between. In most cases we've planned our menus so that the first course or the dessert or both can easily be served in the living room.

The entrée can be the host's show completely. Perhaps he'll carve a roast or turkey if he is skillful with a knife (if not, carve in the kitchen); he can serve side dishes from a warming tray on a table or cart at his side.

When the main course is finished, it is up to you to clear the table and serve the dessert —the host can preside at the coffee maker. Or coffee and dessert can be served later in the living room.

Wine adds festivity to the occasion; if he can be persuaded, your husband might even propose a toast. Such gestures, though not necessary, add a feeling of grace, happy companionability and elegance to even the simplest meal. And this, together with the warmth of host and hostess, forms an ageless tradition—the glow a guest feels when he knows he's truly welcome.

Merrie Old English Dinner

Ham Wellington with Chutney
Baked Sweet Potatoes
Brussels Sprouts and Grapes
Bibb Lettuce Salad
English Trifle
Coffee

HAM WELLINGTON WITH CHUTNEY

1 can (3 pounds) ham
1 stick or ½ packet pie crust mix
1 egg yolk
1 jar (9 ounces) chutney

Heat oven to 425°. Remove gelatin from ham; place ham in greased shallow baking pan.

Prepare pastry for One-crust Pie as directed on package except—roll into rectangle, about 11x10 inches. Place rectangle around *but not under* ham. Trim bottom edges of pastry even with ham; press in to seal.

Beat egg yolk and brush over pastry. Roll left-over pastry 1/8 to 1/16 inch thick; cut into petal or geometric shapes. Arrange shapes in design on top; brush with remaining egg yolk. Bake 30 minutes or until golden brown. Heat chutney; serve with ham.

4 to 6 servings.

BAKED SWEET POTATOES

Wash 4 to 6 small or medium sweet potatoes. Rub skins with shortening and prick with fork. Bake in 425° oven 40 to 50 minutes. Cut criss-cross gash on top; squeeze until potato pops up. Dot potato with butter and sprinkle with salt and pepper.

BRUSSELS SPROUTS AND GRAPES

2 packages (10 ounces each) frozen Brussels sprouts
1½ cups fresh or canned seedless green grapes
2 tablespoons soft butter or margarine

Cook Brussels sprouts as directed on package except—do not drain. Add grapes; cook over low heat 5 minutes longer or until grapes are heated through. Drain; add butter and toss gently.

4 to 6 servings.

BIBB LETTUCE SALAD

2 or 3 medium heads Bibb lettuce or small heads Boston lettuce, washed and chilled
8 to 10 radishes
Bottled oil-and-vinegar salad dressing

Remove center from each lettuce head. Place one center on each of 2 or 3 salad plates; pull leaves out to resemble blossom.

Place an outer section on each remaining salad plate. Push leaves together to resemble blossom. Slice radishes; tuck slices between lettuce leaves. Serve with dressing.

4 to 6 servings.

87

ENGLISH TRIFLE

1 package (18.5 ounces) yellow or pineapple layer cake mix
½ cup raspberry jam
½ cup sherry or, if desired, ⅓ cup orange juice plus 2 tablespoons sherry flavoring
1 can (18 ounces) vanilla ready-to-serve pudding
1 cup chilled whipping cream
¼ cup sugar
¼ cup toasted slivered almonds

Bake cake mix in oblong pan, 13x9x2 inches, as directed on package. Cool. Cut cake crosswise in half. Reserve one half for future use; cut remaining half into 4 squares. Split each square; fill with 2 tablespoons jam. Arrange squares in 2-quart glass serving bowl, cutting squares to fit shape of bowl. Pour wine over cake and allow to soak in a few minutes; spread with pudding. Chill at least 8 hours.

In chilled bowl, beat cream and sugar until stiff; spread over trifle. Sprinkle with almonds.

6 generous servings.

VARIATION

■ *Strawberry Trifle:* Substitute 1 package (16 ounces) frozen strawberry halves, thawed, for the raspberry jam; omit sherry and do not fill cake squares. Arrange half the cake squares in bowl; top with half the strawberries and spread about ½ cup pudding over berries. Repeat.

TIMETABLE

Night before or in the morning:
Make dessert
Prepare salad greens and slice radishes; refrigerate
Prepare sweet potatoes for baking

1 hour before serving:
Prepare Ham Wellington for baking
Bake sweet potatoes
Top dessert with whipped cream and almonds

30 minutes before:
Bake Ham Wellington
Cook Brussels sprouts and grapes
Arrange salads on plates
Make coffee
Heat chutney

FOR YOUR PARTY

A dinner worthy of any holiday is Ham Wellington, a variation of the traditional English beef Wellington. Vary the cut-out decorations to fit the occasion—stars for Christmas, flowers for Easter, hearts for Valentine's Day. For the best effect the meat should be carved in thick slices at the table. If your table is small, use a serving cart for the main part of the meal. Dessert is also an English favorite, a rich combination of wine-soaked cake, jam and whipped cream—called a trifle. Serve this delightful dessert at the table from your prettiest glass bowl.

Dinner with a Fine Italian Hand

Cranberry Rosé or Cranberry Punch
Ham and Melon Appetizers
Lemon Veal Scaloppine
Noodles Alfredo   Zucchini Fans
Italian Relish Salad
Bread Sticks
Baked Alaska Spumoni Pie
Espresso

CRANBERRY ROSÉ

2 cups rosé, chilled
1 cup cranberry cocktail, chilled
2 cups carbonated water, chilled

Just before serving, stir together wine, cranberry cocktail and carbonated water; pour over ice. If desired, garnish with lemon or orange slices.

6 servings (about ¾ cup each).

CRANBERRY PUNCH

1 bottle (32 ounces) cranberry cocktail, chilled
2 bottles (7 ounces each) ginger ale, chilled
3 tablespoons lemon juice

Just before serving, stir together all ingredients; pour over ice.

6 servings (about 1 cup each).

VARIATION

■ *Cranberry Grape Punch:* Substitute 1 cup grape juice for the ginger ale and lemon juice.

HAM AND MELON APPETIZERS

1 eggplant
¼ pound thinly sliced prosciutto or boiled ham
½ cantaloupe
¼ honeydew melon

Cut thin slice from bottom of eggplant so it will stand upright. Place eggplant on serving tray. Cut ham into 3x1-inch strips. Scoop balls from melons or cut melons into ½-inch cubes. On each plastic or wooden pick, place one melon ball and thread one ham strip. Insert picks in eggplant.

6 servings.

Note: This appetizer can be assembled in advance and refrigerated up to 3 hours.

VARIATION

■ *Ham and Vegetable Appetizers:* Substitute cherry tomatoes and drained marinated artichoke hearts for the melons.

89

LEMON VEAL SCALOPPINE

2 pounds veal round steak, ¼ inch
  thick, or 6 veal cutlets (about
  4 ounces each)
½ cup all-purpose flour
2 teaspoons garlic salt
⅓ cup butter or margarine
6 lemon slices
1 teaspoon instant beef bouillon
½ cup hot water
2 tablespoons lemon juice

Cut meat into 6 serving pieces; if necessary, pound meat until ¼ inch thick. Stir together flour and garlic salt; coat meat with flour mixture. Melt butter in large skillet; brown meat over medium heat 5 to 7 minutes on each side.

Place meat in ungreased baking dish, 13½x9x2 inches. Top each piece with lemon slice. (Or place lemon slices on veal at serving time.) Cover and refrigerate.

Heat oven to 350°. Dissolve bouillon in water. Add lemon juice; pour over meat. Cover and bake 25 to 30 minutes.

6 servings.

NOODLES ALFREDO

10 ounces fine noodles
½ cup butter or margarine
½ cup light cream
½ cup grated Parmesan cheese
½ teaspoon salt
  Dash pepper

Cook noodles as directed on package. While noodles cook, heat butter and cream over low heat until butter is melted. Stir in cheese, salt and pepper; keep warm over low heat.

Drain noodles; return hot noodles to kettle. Pour sauce over noodles, gently tossing until noodles are well coated.

6 servings.

ZUCCHINI FANS

6 medium zucchini (about 2 pounds)
2 tablespoons soft butter or margarine
  Salt
  Paprika

Remove ends of zucchini but do not pare. Heat 1 inch salted water (½ teaspoon salt to 1 cup water) to boiling. Add zucchini. Cover and heat to boiling; cook 8 to 10 minutes. Drain.

Cut each zucchini lengthwise into 3 or 4 slices to within 1½ inches of one end. Place in shallow pan. Carefully spread slices to resemble fan; brush with butter. Cover and refrigerate.

Sprinkle zucchini slices with salt and paprika. Set oven control at broil and/or 550°. Broil 4 inches from heat 3 to 5 minutes or until heated through.

6 servings.

ITALIAN RELISH SALAD

2 jars (6 ounces each) marinated
  artichoke hearts, drained
18 cherry tomatoes
1 can (3 ounces) sliced mushrooms,
  drained
1 can (6 ounces) pitted ripe olives,
  drained
  Spinach leaves
  Vinegar
  Salad oil

On each salad plate arrange artichoke hearts, cherry tomatoes, mushroom slices and olives on spinach. Serve vinegar and salad oil in separate containers.

6 servings.

Use uncooked manicotti for napkin rings.

Lemon Veal Scaloppine and Zucchini Fans share the platter.

Bread sticks and chili peppers served in a wine basket.

Italian Relish Salad—to please the eye and palate.

Espresso is a perfect accompaniment for the pie.

BAKED ALASKA SPUMONI PIE

1 stick or ½ packet pie crust mix
**1 pint each strawberry, pistachio and
    chocolate ice cream**
    Meringue (below)

Bake 9-inch baked pie shell as directed on package. Cool. (For a firmer pie shell, place in freezer about 30 minutes before filling.) Working quickly, pack scoops of ice cream, alternating flavors, in pie shell. Freeze until firm.

Heat oven to 500°. Heap Meringue onto ice cream; spread over ice cream, carefully sealing to edge of crust. Bake 3 to 5 minutes or until top is a delicate brown. Serve immediately or place in freezer.

MERINGUE

3 egg whites
¼ teaspoon cream of tartar
6 tablespoons sugar
½ teaspoon vanilla

Beat egg whites and cream of tartar until foamy. Beat in sugar, 1 tablespoon at a time; continue beating until stiff and glossy. *Do not underbeat.* Beat in vanilla.

Note: Pie can be frozen up to 1 month. After baking, immediately place pie in box, then wrap box and freeze. Fifteen minutes before serving, remove pie from freezer.

TIMETABLE

Night before or in the morning:
  Make pie
  Prepare zucchini; refrigerate
  Prepare meat; refrigerate
  Chill wine and cranberry cocktail
  Cut ham into strips and scoop melon
    balls; refrigerate

1 hour before serving:
  Assemble Ham and Melon Appetizers;
    serve with Cranberry Rosé when
    guests arrive
  Arrange salads on plates; refrigerate

30 minutes before:
  Pour hot bouillon mixture over veal;
    bake
  Cook noodles and prepare sauce
  Make coffee

About 5 minutes before:
  Broil zucchini
  Drain noodles; stir in sauce

Note: Remove dessert from freezer about 15 minutes before serving

FOR YOUR PARTY

Keynote of this Italian dinner is an interesting play of patterns—the ham and melon appetizers arrayed on an eggplant, the notched lemon slices topping the meat, the fan-shaped zucchini. The zucchini can do double duty, as a vegetable and a garnish for the veal. And, for still further pattern-play, use a wine basket for a centerpiece. It's an imaginative holder for chili peppers, grape leaves and bread sticks; for additional interest, you could surround it with fat white candles or votive lights.

St. Tropez
Seafood Dinner

Clam-Tomato Juice on the Rocks
Seafood Coquilles
Buttered Broccoli
Celery Victor
French Rolls
Strawberry Crêpes
Coffee

CLAM-TOMATO JUICE ON THE ROCKS

Chill 1 bottle (32 ounces) clam and tomato juice. Just before serving, pour over ice into glasses. Serve with a green onion or carrot-stick stirrer in each glass.

5 or 6 servings (¾ cup each).

TIMETABLE

Night before or in the morning:
Chill juice for appetizer
Thaw scallops and soup in refrigerator
Prepare Celery Victor
Make crêpes and prepare strawberries

1 hour before serving:
Fill crêpes with sour cream mixture
Wrap rolls in foil
Prepare Seafood Coquilles for baking

20 minutes before:
Bake Seafood Coquilles
Cook 2 packages (10 ounces each) frozen broccoli spears
Arrange Celery Victor on salad plates
Place rolls in oven for 10 minutes
Make coffee
Heat crêpes

SEAFOOD COQUILLES

1 package (12 ounces) frozen scallops, thawed, drained and quartered
1 package (10 ounces) frozen cooked shrimp, thawed and drained
1 can (6 ounces) sliced mushrooms, drained
1 can (10¾ ounces) condensed cream of shrimp soup
1 tablespoon grated lemon peel (½ lemon)
1 tablespoon chopped chives
Grated Parmesan cheese or French fried onion rings

Heat oven to 400° Mix thoroughly all ingredients except cheese. Place about 1 cup mixture in each of 5 or 6 baking shells or individual casseroles.

Place shells on baking sheet. Bake 15 minutes. Remove from oven; top shells with cheese and bake 2 to 3 minutes longer.

5 or 6 servings.

VARIATION

■ *Seafood Coquilles with Potatoes:* Before baking, prepare instant mashed potato puffs as directed on package for 4 servings. Place potatoes in pastry tube; pipe mixture around edge of each filled baking shell. Sprinkle with paprika or grated Parmesan cheese.

93

CELERY VICTOR

2 cans (16 ounces each) celery hearts,
    drained
2 medium tomatoes, cut into 10 to 12
    wedges
½ cup bottled Italian salad dressing
    Bibb lettuce
    Pitted ripe olives

Place celery hearts and tomato wedges in baking dish, 8x8x2 inches; pour salad dressing over vegetables. Cover; refrigerate at least 2 hours.

On each salad plate, arrange celery hearts and tomato wedges on lettuce. Drizzle with remaining salad dressing. Garnish with olives.

5 or 6 servings.

VARIATION

■ *Artichoke-Tomato Salad:* Substitute 1 can (14 ounces) artichoke hearts, drained, for the celery hearts.

FOR YOUR PARTY

Your guests will never guess that this gourmet menu is composed almost entirely of canned, frozen and packaged ingredients. Serve the Seafood Coquilles in scallop shells or shell-shaped dishes. (*Coquille* is the French word for shell.) Make quick work of the traditional Celery Victor salad by using canned celery hearts. And as for dessert, be dramatic. Serve the warm crêpes with a flaming sauce in front of guests.

STRAWBERRY CREPES

1 cup buttermilk baking mix
1 egg
1 cup milk
2 cups fresh strawberries
½ cup granulated sugar
1 cup dairy sour cream
⅓ cup brown sugar (packed)

Beat baking mix, egg and milk with rotary beater until smooth. Lightly grease a 6- or 7-inch skillet. Heat skillet until few drops water sprinkled on it "skitter" around. Pour 2 tablespoons batter into hot skillet; rotate pan until batter covers bottom. Cook until light brown; turn and brown on other side. Place crêpes between paper towels until ready to fill. (Crêpes can be prepared several hours ahead. Stack and cover.)

Slice strawberries; sprinkle with granulated sugar. Cover and refrigerate. Mix sour cream and brown sugar. Place 1 tablespoon sour cream mixture on each crêpe; roll up and place seam side down on ovenproof serving platter. Cover with aluminum foil.

When main course is served, turn off oven. Heat crêpes during meal. Serve warm with sweetened strawberries.

12 to 15 crêpes.

Note: To flame, heat sweetened strawberries in chafing dish just until warm. Warm 2 tablespoons orange-flavored liqueur or brandy; pour over strawberries and ignite.

Timesaver

Substitute 2 packages (10 ounces each) frozen strawberries, thawed, for the strawberries and granulated sugar.

An elegant centerpiece—glass balls and shells on coral.

Celery Victor—a cool beginning for dinner.

Seafood Coquilles with Potatoes.

Serve the crêpes in the den or living room.

Mexican Dinner— Bright and Spicy

Guacamole Dip with Tacos
or Black Bean Dip
Mexicali Chicken
Artichoke Hearts in Tomato Rice
Shredded Tossed Greens
Tortillas with Salsa Jalapeña
Mexican Wedding Cakes
Tijuana Chocolate or Mexican Chocolate

GUACAMOLE DIP WITH TACOS

1 can (7¾ ounces) frozen avocado dip
(guacamole), thawed
¼ teaspoon cumin
4 drops red pepper sauce
1 package (5½ ounces) frozen
cocktail tacos
Lettuce

Blend avocado dip, cumin and pepper sauce. Place in small bowl. Heat tacos as directed on package. Arrange tacos on lettuce-lined serving plate. Serve with dip.

4 or 5 servings.

BLACK BEAN DIP

1 can (11 ounces) condensed
black bean soup
1 can (8 ounces) tomato sauce
½ cup shredded natural Cheddar cheese
¼ teaspoon chili powder
Snacks

Combine soup, tomato sauce, cheese and chili powder in small saucepan; heat through, stirring constantly. Serve with snacks.

About 2 cups.

MEXICALI CHICKEN

2½- to 3-pound broiler-fryer chicken,
cut up
2 tablespoons salad oil
1 bottle (7 ounces) spicy sauce for tacos
½ cup water
1 teaspoon salt
½ teaspoon oregano
¼ teaspoon instant minced garlic
¼ cup instant minced onion
2 cups shredded Cheddar cheese
(about 8 ounces)

Wash chicken and pat dry. Heat oil in large skillet. Cook chicken in oil over medium heat about 15 minutes or until brown on all sides. Drain off fat. Mix sauce for tacos, water, salt, oregano, instant garlic and instant onion. Pour over chicken. Reduce heat. Cover; simmer 30 minutes or until chicken is tender. Place chicken in ungreased baking pan, 9x9x2 inches, or in ovenproof serving dish. Cool. Sprinkle with cheese; cover and refrigerate.

Heat oven to 400°. Bake 30 to 40 minutes or until hot, removing cover last 20 minutes.

4 or 5 servings.

Note: If spicy sauce for tacos is not available, omit water and mix 1 can (8 ounces) tomato sauce, 1 teaspoon chili powder, 5 drops red pepper sauce and 2 tablespoons vinegar.

A south-of-the-border feast with a surprise centerpiece—a Mexican tin lamp (lit from within by a flashlight) that doubles as a "vase" for bright paper flowers.

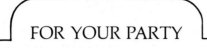

FOR YOUR PARTY

To set a south-of-the-border scene let your color sense run riot in decoration. Mingle all the hot Mexican shades of yellow, orange, pink and red with cool notes of green. We've chosen a deep gold cloth, orange plates and napkins and green glassware. The centerpiece is a typical example of Mexican pierced tin, a lamp we've lighted from within by a small flashlight and covered with Mexican paper flowers at the top and base. (Tin work and flowers are available at large department stores and Mexican specialty shops throughout the country.) Use colorful pottery dishes and wooden bowls for the spicy Mexican food. The miniature tacos and Guacamole (Gwah-kah-móh-leh) Dip can be served in the living room—or you might want to substitute crisp tortilla (tohr-téh-l'yah) chips with Black Bean Dip. The chicken is pepped up with a spicy sauce usually used for tacos. We've included tortillas, a staple of the Mexican diet, in place of bread. They're rolled around salsa jalapeña (ha-la-páy-nyo), a very hot chili relish. And finally the Mexican Wedding Cakes, actually rich nutty cookies, and Tijuana Chocolate—a marvelous mixture of espresso, brandy and chocolate ice cream—bring the meal to a delicious climax. Pyramid the cookies on a serving plate and let your guests drink-and-spoon the chocolate from mugs.

ARTICHOKE HEARTS IN TOMATO RICE

    1 can (14 ounces) artichoke hearts
    1 can (16 ounces) stewed tomatoes
    1½ cups uncooked instant rice
    1 tablespoon dried shredded green
      onion or 3 fresh green onions,
      cut up
    ¼ teaspoon salt

Combine artichoke hearts (with liquid), tomatoes, rice, onion and salt in large skillet. Heat to boiling, stirring frequently. Reduce heat. Cover; simmer 10 minutes or until rice is tender.

4 or 5 servings.

SHREDDED TOSSED GREENS

    1 medium head lettuce, washed and
      chilled
    1 medium green pepper, finely chopped
    1 small red onion, thinly sliced and
      separated into rings
    ½ cup bottled oil-and-vinegar salad
      dressing
    ⅛ teaspoon chili powder

Shred lettuce with knife. Place in large plastic bag. Add green pepper and onion rings and refrigerate.

Just before serving, mix salad dressing and chili powder; pour into bag. Close bag and shake until vegetables are coated with dressing. Pour into salad bowl.

4 or 5 servings.

TORTILLAS
WITH SALSA JALAPEÑA

1 package (10 ounces) frozen tortillas
  Soft butter or margarine
  Salsa jalapeña (hot chili relish)

Heat oven to 400°. Separate tortillas into 2 equal stacks. Wrap each stack in aluminum foil. Heat 20 minutes. Guests spread tortillas with butter and salsa jalapeña, then roll them up and eat as a bread.

4 or 5 servings.

MEXICAN WEDDING CAKES

1 cup butter or margarine, softened
½ cup confectioners' sugar
1 teaspoon vanilla
2¼ cups all-purpose flour*
¼ teaspoon salt
¼ cup finely chopped nuts

Heat oven to 400°. Mix thoroughly butter, sugar and vanilla. Work in flour, salt and nuts until dough holds together. Shape dough into 1-inch balls. Place on ungreased baking sheet.

Bake 10 to 12 minutes or until set but not brown. While warm, roll in confectioners' sugar. Cool. Roll in sugar again.

About 4 dozen cookies.

Do not use self-rising flour in this recipe.

VARIATION

■ *Ambrosia Balls:* Omit nuts; add 1 cup finely cut coconut and 1 tablespoon grated orange peel with the flour.

TIJUANA CHOCOLATE

For each serving, stir together 1 teaspoon instant espresso coffee, ⅛ teaspoon cinnamon and 1 ounce (2 tablespoons) brandy in mug. Pour in boiling water to fill mug ⅔ full. Top with scoop of chocolate ice cream.

MEXICAN CHOCOLATE

3 ounces unsweetened chocolate
½ cup sugar
3 tablespoons powdered instant coffee
1 teaspoon cinnamon
½ teaspoon nutmeg
¼ teaspoon salt
1½ cups water
4 cups milk
  Whipped cream

Heat chocolate, sugar, coffee, spices, salt and water over low heat, stirring until mixture is smooth. Heat to boiling; reduce heat and simmer 4 minutes, stirring constantly.

Stir in milk; heat. Beat with rotary beater until foamy. Top with whipped cream.

4 or 5 servings (about 1 cup each).

TIMETABLE

Night before or in the morning:
  Thaw avocado dip
  Bake Mexican Wedding Cakes
  Cook chicken; refrigerate
  Prepare salad ingredients

40 minutes before serving:
  Place chicken in oven
  Wrap tortillas in foil
  Heat tacos and prepare avocado dip;
    serve when guests arrive

20 minutes before:
  Heat tortillas
  Cook Artichoke Hearts in Tomato Rice
  Toss salad
  Prepare chocolate just before serving
    dessert

99

Mideast Feast

> Cucumber Soup
> Roast Rack of Lamb
> Minted Pears
> Bulgur Pilaf
> Buttered Carrots
> Hot Spinach Salad
> Cream Puffs with Chocolate Sauce
> Coffee

CUCUMBER SOUP

2 medium cucumbers
1½ cups buttermilk
1 teaspoon salt
⅛ teaspoon pepper
1 teaspoon instant minced onion

Wash one cucumber but do not pare; cut 4 to 6 thin slices and reserve for garnish. Pare remaining cucumber and cut both cucumbers into ¾-inch slices.

Pour ¼ cup of the buttermilk into blender container; add half the cucumber slices and blend on high speed until smooth. Add remaining slices, the salt, pepper and onion. Blend until smooth, about 1 minute. Stir in remaining buttermilk. Chill. Serve in cups and garnish each with reserved cucumber slice.

4 to 6 servings (about ½ cup each).

VARIATIONS
When adding remaining cucumber slices, add one of the following:

1 teaspoon lemon juice
2 teaspoons horseradish
1 teaspoon Worcestershire sauce

ROAST RACK OF LAMB

2 racks of lamb (2 to 3 pounds each)
2 teaspoons marjoram
1 teaspoon garlic salt
2 tablespoons Worcestershire sauce
1 cup bottled oil-and-vinegar salad dressing
Mint leaves
1 jar (14 ounces) pear halves in mint flavoring

Heat oven to 375°. Have meat retailer saw backbone of lamb between center rib bones so meat can easily be cut for serving. Place racks of lamb fat side up in shallow roasting pan. Insert meat thermometer so tip is in thickest part of meat and does not rest on fat or bone. Do not add water. Do not cover.

Combine marjoram, garlic salt, Worcestershire sauce and salad dressing; brush racks of lamb with mixture. Roast meat 30 minutes; brush again with salad dressing. Roast 30 minutes longer or until thermometer registers 180° (for medium doneness). Remove meat to warm platter; garnish with mint leaves and, if desired, pear halves.

4 to 6 servings.

Note: When purchasing meat, specify the number of ribs needed, about 2 or 3 ribs per person. To serve, cut between each 2 or 3 ribs.

Show-off service: The talented host carves and serves the Rack of Lamb at the table.

BULGUR PILAF

2 tablespoons butter
1 cup bulgur wheat
1 teaspoon instant minced onion
2 cups chicken broth*
½ teaspoon salt
¼ teaspoon oregano
  Dash pepper

Melt butter in medium skillet. Add bulgur wheat; cook and stir until wheat is golden. Stir in remaining ingredients. Cover; heat to boiling. Reduce heat; simmer 15 minutes.

4 to 6 servings.

° *Chicken broth can be made by dissolving 2 chicken bouillon cubes in 2 cups boiling water, or use canned chicken broth.*

FOR YOUR PARTY

Surprise your company with a menu slightly mideastern in flavor: cold cucumber soup, a garlic-flavored rack of lamb, bulgur pilaf (made from cracked wheat) and a bacon-flavored hot spinach salad. For easy handling, serve the soup in mugs, garnished with cucumber slices, in the living room. Surround the lamb with mint leaves, and prepare the spinach salad at a side table or on a serving cart. Toss it in a chafing dish and serve on individual salad plates.

BUTTERED CARROTS

Prepare 2 packages (10 ounces each) carrot nuggets frozen in butter sauce in cooking pouch as directed on package.

4 to 6 servings.

HOT SPINACH SALAD

16 ounces spinach
½ cup bottled oil-and-vinegar salad dressing
2 tablespoons imitation bacon chips

Wash spinach and remove stems; dry leaves. Tear leaves into bite-size pieces. Place greens in large plastic bags and refrigerate.

Just before serving, heat salad dressing in chafing dish. Add spinach and bacon chips; toss until greens are well coated.

4 to 6 servings.

Note: If preparing the salad at the table, toss half the spinach leaves at a time—that's as much as a regular-size chafing dish holds.

While the host carves, the hostess prepares the salad.

CREAM PUFFS WITH CHOCOLATE SAUCE

1 cup water
½ cup butter or margarine
1 cup all-purpose flour
4 eggs
    French Whipped Cream (below)
½ can (16.5-ounce size) chocolate ready-to-spread frosting

Heat oven to 400°. In small saucepan, heat water and butter to a rolling boil. Stir in flour. Stir vigorously over low heat until mixture forms a ball, about 1 minute. Remove from heat. Beat in eggs, all at one time; continue beating until smooth. Drop dough by ¼ cupfuls 3 inches apart onto ungreased baking sheet. Bake 35 to 40 minutes or until puffed and golden. Cool on wire rack.

Just before serving, cut off tops of 4 to 6 puffs. (Freeze remaining puffs for future use.) Pull out any filaments of soft dough. Fill puffs with French Whipped Cream; replace tops. Heat chocolate ready-to-spread frosting over low heat, stirring frequently. Top puffs with chocolate sauce.

4 to 6 puffs.

FRENCH WHIPPED CREAM

In chilled bowl, beat 1 cup chilled whipping cream until stiff. Gently fold in ¼ cup crème de cacao.

About 2 cups.

VARIATIONS

■ *Ice-cream Puffs:* Omit French Whipped Cream and fill puffs with 1 pint French vanilla, peppermint or coffee ice cream.

■ *Pudding Puffs:* Omit French Whipped Cream and fill puffs with 1 can (18 ounces) vanilla or 1 can (17.5 ounces) chocolate ready-to-serve pudding.

■ *Candy Fluff Puffs:* Omit crème de cacao in French Whipped Cream and fold in ½ cup crushed peppermint stick candy.

Note: To freeze cream puffs before baking, place baking sheet with mounds of dough uncovered in freezer and freeze until solid, about 4 hours. Remove from freezer; with spatula, quickly loosen puffs and place in large freezer bag. Seal bag and store in freezer until ready to bake. (Puffs can be frozen up to 1 month.)

To bake, heat oven to 400°. Place desired number of frozen puffs 3 inches apart on ungreased baking sheet; bake 45 to 50 minutes.

TIMETABLE

Night before or in the morning:
  Bake cream puffs
  Prepare soup; chill
  Prepare spinach for salad

1 hour 15 minutes before serving:
  Roast lamb

30 minutes before:
  Cook carrots
  Cook pilaf
  Fill cream puffs; refrigerate
  Make coffee
  Heat salad dressing; toss salad

Treat of Treats— Tenderloin

Marinated Relishes
Roast Beef Tenderloin
Oven-browned Potatoes
Asparagus Almondine
Tomatoes Vinaigrette
Dinner Rolls
Bananas Flambé
Coffee

MARINATED RELISHES

1 jar (8 ounces) pickled mushrooms
1 jar (8 ounces) pickled baby corn
1 can (6 ounces) pitted ripe olives
   Lettuce

Chill mushrooms, corn and olives; drain. On serving tray, arrange vegetables and olives on lettuce. Serve immediately or refrigerate until serving time.

6 to 8 servings.

TIMETABLE

Night before or in the morning:
  Prepare Tomatoes Vinaigrette
  Chill relishes
  Wrap rolls in foil
  Prepare ice-cream balls; freeze

1 hour 15 minutes before serving:
  Roast tenderloin
  Arrange relishes on serving plate; serve
   when guests arrive
  Arrange salads on plates; refrigerate
  Prepare and bake potatoes
  Assemble dessert ingredients

15 minutes before:
  Cook asparagus
  Make coffee
  Heat rolls

ROAST BEEF TENDERLOIN

Brush 3- to 4-pound beef tenderloin with melted butter or margarine. Place on rack in broiler pan; insert meat thermometer so tip is in thickest part of meat. Roast in 425° oven 45 to 60 minutes or until thermometer registers 140° (rare).

6 to 8 servings.

Note: Roasts are easier to carve if allowed to set 15 to 20 minutes after removing from oven. Since meat continues to cook after removal from oven, if roast is to "set," it should be removed from oven when thermometer registers 5 to 10° lower than the desired doneness.

VARIATION

■ *Mock Tenderloin:* Substitute 3- to 4-pound eye-of-the-round roast for tenderloin. Rub meat tenderizer over roast as directed by manufacturer. Roast about 1 hour or until meat thermometer registers 140° (rare) or 160° (medium).

OVEN-BROWNED POTATOES

8 to 10 baking potatoes
½ cup butter or margarine, melted
Salt

Heat oven to 425°. Pare potatoes; brush each with butter and sprinkle with salt. Place around meat on rack in broiler pan. Cook 40 minutes or until tender and golden brown, basting occasionally with butter.

6 to 8 servings.

VARIATIONS

■ *Fan Tan Potatoes:* Cut each pared potato lengthwise into ⅛-inch slices, being careful not to cut completely through one end. Spread slices to resemble fan; brush with butter and sprinkle with salt.

■ *Cross-cut Potatoes:* Cut each pared potato diagonally into ½-inch slices, being careful not to cut completely through bottom; repeat in opposite direction. Brush with butter and sprinkle with salt.

Fan Tan Potatoes—attractive and easy.

ASPARAGUS ALMONDINE

2 packages (10 ounces each) frozen asparagus spears
2 tablespoons soft butter or margarine
¼ cup roasted slivered almonds

Cook asparagus spears as directed on package. Turn into serving dish; dot with butter and sprinkle with almonds.

6 to 8 servings.

FOR YOUR PARTY

Beef tenderloin is almost everyone's idea of a super party entrée. Besides tasting marvelous it yields several bonuses to the hostess. It cooks in a short time, requires no split-second attention, is easy for even a rank amateur to carve, and always comes out tender. It should be crusty brown on the outside, rare inside, and served in thick slices. Serve the end portion to those who like their beef a little better done. The relishes can be prepared in minutes; they look especially festive if you serve them surrounding a big tomato studded with picks for spearing. Use the Fan Tan Potatoes and sprigs of watercress or parsley to garnish the meat platter and let the host carve and serve at the table. The Bananas Flambé make a dramatic climax flamed at the table in a chafing dish.

TOMATOES VINAIGRETTE

6 medium tomatoes
½ cup bottled oil-and-vinegar salad
   dressing or Clear French Dressing (below)
   Instant minced onion
   Parsley flakes
   Lettuce cups

Cut each tomato into 3 or 4 slices; arrange slices in baking dish, 13½x9x2 inches. Pour salad dressing over tomatoes and sprinkle with onion and parsley flakes. Cover and refrigerate at least 2 hours.

Place lettuce cup on each salad plate; arrange 2 or 3 tomato slices in each and drizzle with salad dressing left in baking dish.

6 to 8 servings.

CLEAR FRENCH DRESSING

 ½ cup salad oil
 ¼ cup vinegar
 1 tablespoon sugar
1½ teaspoons salt
 ¼ teaspoon celery seed
 ¼ teaspoon dry mustard
 ⅛ teaspoon grated onion
 1 small clove garlic, peeled

Mix all ingredients except garlic. Add garlic; let stand in dressing about 1 hour. Remove garlic.

¾ cup dressing.

BANANAS FLAMBÉ

1 quart vanilla ice cream
½ cup butter or margarine
⅔ cup brown sugar (packed)
1 teaspoon cinnamon
4 firm medium bananas
⅓ cup white rum
6 to 8 maraschino cherries (with stems)

Scoop ice cream into balls; arrange balls in baking pan, 9x9x2 inches, and place in freezer.

Just before serving, melt butter and sugar with cinnamon in chafing dish or saucepan. Cook over medium-high heat, stirring occasionally, until golden brown, about 3 minutes. Remove ice-cream balls from freezer; place in dessert dishes.

Into chafing dish, cut bananas diagonally into ½-inch slices. Heat through, carefully turning slices to coat. Heat rum until warm; pour over slices and ignite. Spoon sauce and banana slices over ice-cream balls. Garnish each serving with a cherry.

6 to 8 servings.

FLAMING TIPS

Considering how spectacular it can be to flame foods in front of guests, it's really surprising how simple they are to make. Insure success by using 80-proof liquors. Some favorites—rum, brandy and orange-flavored or cherry-flavored liqueurs.

The food should be hot but the liquor should be heated until just warm. If it boils, the alcohol will evaporate and the liquor won't flame.

Pour the warmed liquor into the center of the hot food and, without stirring, ignite with a long fireplace match. Always light the dish at the table—don't try to carry it flaming from the kitchen.

Chicken Dinner Elegante

Fruit Kabobs with Catawba
Chicken in Mushroom-Sauterne Sauce
Oven-baked Rice
Artichokes with Lemon Butter
Cucumber-Tomato Vinaigrette
Dinner Rolls
Ice-cream Bombe
Coffee

FRUIT KABOBS WITH CATAWBA

½ pint fresh strawberries
1 can (11 ounces) mandarin orange
  segments
1 large banana
1 large orange or grapefruit
1 bottle (25.6 ounces) sparkling catawba
  grape juice, chilled

Wash strawberries but do not remove hulls or stems. Drain mandarin orange segments, reserving syrup. Cut banana into ½-inch slices. Pour reserved mandarin orange syrup over banana slices.

On 4- to 5-inch bamboo skewers, place a strawberry, banana slice and mandarin orange segment. Insert skewers in orange. (If necessary, cut thin slice from bottom of orange so it will stand level.) Pour grape juice into stemmed glasses; serve with kabobs.

6 to 8 servings.

Note: Other fruits such as melon balls or pieces, pineapple chunks, pitted dark sweet cherries or seedless green grapes can be substituted for the strawberries, banana and orange segments. Champagne or sauterne can be substituted for the grape juice.

CHICKEN IN MUSHROOM-SAUTERNE SAUCE

6 to 8 large chicken breast halves
1 can (10¾ ounces) condensed cream
  of mushroom soup
1 can (3 ounces) sliced mushrooms,
  drained
1 envelope (about 1½ ounces) onion
  soup mix
⅔ cup sauterne
1 jar (2 ounces) pimiento, drained

Wash chicken breasts and pat dry. Place skin side up in ungreased baking pan, 13x9x2 inches. Stir together soup, mushrooms, soup mix and wine; spread over chicken pieces. Cover and refrigerate.

Heat oven to 425°. Bake covered 30 minutes. Uncover and bake 20 minutes longer or until tender. If necessary, spoon excess fat from sauce. Place chicken breasts on warm platter; spoon about half the sauce over chicken. Cut pimiento into narrow strips; arrange on chicken. Serve remaining sauce with chicken.

6 to 8 servings.

Today's Sit-down Dinners

Our do-it-yourself Mushroom Centerpiece.

Space-saver: The bowl of rice shares the chicken platter.

A black tray is a perfect foil for the kabobs.

Provide small plates for the discarded leaves.

Our attention-getting dessert—garnished with kumquats.

OVEN-BAKED RICE

**2 packages (6 ounces each) seasoned
  long grain and wild rice
5 cups boiling water**

Heat oven to 425°. Mix ingredients thoroughly in ungreased 3-quart casserole or baking dish, 13x9x2 inches. Cover tightly; bake 45 minutes or until liquid is absorbed and rice is tender.

6 to 8 generous servings.

ARTICHOKES
WITH LEMON BUTTER

**6 quarts water
2 tablespoons lemon juice
1 teaspoon salt
3 or 4 small artichokes
  Lemon Butter (below)**

In large kettle, heat water, lemon juice and salt to boiling. Slice 1 inch off top of each artichoke; discard top. Snip off points of remaining leaves with scissors. Trim stem even with base of artichoke; cut each artichoke lengthwise in half. Place in kettle; heat to boiling.

Reduce heat; cover and simmer 30 to 40 minutes. (Artichokes are done when leaves pull off easily and bottom is tender when pierced with knife.) Remove artichokes carefully from water; drain. Serve hot with Lemon Butter.

6 to 8 servings.

LEMON BUTTER

**1 cup butter or margarine
1 tablespoon plus 1 teaspoon
  grated lemon peel
½ cup lemon juice**

Heat all ingredients in small saucepan over low heat until butter is melted.

About 1½ cups.

FOR YOUR PARTY

Artichokes are traditionally served as a separate course on special artichoke plates with sections for the discarded leaves. However, just in case your china cupboard doesn't include artichoke plates, we've halved the vegetable so it can be easily served along with the chicken and rice on the dinner plate, with a small plate provided for the leaves. To eat, begin with outer leaves; twist off one at a time and dip the tender fleshy part in lemon butter. Then draw the buttered portion between your teeth; discard the leaf. After the leaves have been removed cut off the spiny choke and eat the smooth round bottom portion, considered a great delicacy. To make the unusual Mushroom Centerpiece, start the day before your party—the mushrooms take time to dry. Insert 3-inch pieces of wire in 10 to 15 fresh mushrooms of varying sizes; spray with silver paint and dry thoroughly. (Mushrooms will gradually shrink and alter their shape as they dry.) Place a needle frog in a wicker basket (florist's clay underneath frog will help to secure it); cut a piece of styrofoam slightly smaller than the top of the basket and place firmly on the frog. Cover with moss. Insert painted dried mushrooms on wires at random in the moss-covered styrofoam; intersperse with tiny strawflowers, mimosa or baby's breath. This centerpiece is guaranteed to be a conversation piece!

CUCUMBER-TOMATO VINAIGRETTE

3 medium tomatoes
2 medium cucumbers
½ cup bottled oil-and-vinegar salad
   dressing
   Curly endive
6 to 8 tablespoons dairy sour cream
6 to 8 teaspoons red or black caviar

Cut each tomato into 8 wedges; arrange in baking dish, 9x9x2 inches. Into baking dish, cut unpared cucumber diagonally into ¼-inch slices. Pour salad dressing over vegetables. Cover and refrigerate at least 2 hours.

Arrange tomatoes, cucumber slices and endive on salad plates. Drizzle with remaining salad dressing. Spoon 1 tablespoon sour cream on each salad; top with 1 teaspoon caviar.

6 to 8 servings.

TIMETABLE

Several days before:
   Make Ice-cream Bombe
Night before or in the morning:
   Prepare Cucumber-Tomato Vinaigrette
   Unmold Ice-cream Bombe; return to
      freezer
   Wrap rolls in foil
   Combine ingredients for Lemon Butter;
      refrigerate
   Prepare chicken for baking; refrigerate
1 hour before serving:
   Arrange salads on plates; refrigerate
   Bake chicken
   Prepare and bake rice
   Cook artichokes
   Prepare Fruit Kabobs; serve with catawba
      when guests arrive
10 minutes before:
   Place rolls in oven
   Make coffee
   Heat Lemon Butter
Note: Remove dessert from freezer about
15 minutes before serving

ICE-CREAM BOMBE

2 pints orange sherbet
1 pint pistachio ice cream
1 pint chocolate ice cream

Slightly soften 1 pint of the orange sherbet; spoon into chilled 1½- to 2-quart metal mold or bowl. Freeze at least 1 hour or until firm. Slightly soften pistachio ice cream; spread over orange sherbet in mold. Freeze until firm. Repeat with chocolate ice cream and remaining orange sherbet. Cover mold with waxed paper; freeze until firm.

To unmold, turn mold onto chilled serving plate. Dip a cloth into hot water; wring out and place over top of mold just a few minutes. Lift off mold. If desired, decorate ice-cream mold with kumquats and pressurized cream. Return to freezer; remove 15 to 30 minutes before serving.

8 to 10 servings.

Note: For a different effect, spread 2 pints of orange sherbet on bottom and side of mold; freeze. Repeat with pistachio and chocolate ice cream.

VARIATIONS
Substitute one of the following combinations:

- Pistachio, butter pecan, orange sherbet
- Chocolate, French vanilla, coffee
- Strawberry, pistachio, chocolate
- Cherry, chocolate chip, chocolate
- Peppermint, vanilla, chocolate
- Pistachio, dark cherry, coffee

Brittany Farm Supper

Cheese and Crackers
Coq au Vin
Salad Provence   French Rolls
Grapes and Pineapple in Sour Cream
or Strawberries to Dip
Coffee

CHEESE AND CRACKERS

Arrange wedges of blue cheese and Camembert cheese on cheese board with crackers. Serve with cranberry cocktail or, if desired, with sherry or vermouth.

FOR YOUR PARTY

If you spend your nine-to-five hours in an office or engaged in some other busy activity, you may think that week-night entertaining is out for you. But this dinner —borrowed from French country cooking —can literally be on the table in twenty minutes. The secret is to make the Coq au Vin the night before and merely reheat it while you're assembling the salad and dessert and warming the rolls. Serve the main dish in large shallow soup bowls —great for dunking the crusty bread. Or if you have small soup bowls, put the broth in these and the chicken on a dinner plate. Use your most attractive glass dessert dishes for the fruit and sour cream. Plug an electric coffee maker in near the table and ask a guest to pour coffee while you serve dessert.

COQ AU VIN

2½- to 3-pound broiler-fryer chicken,
    cut up
6 slices bacon
½ cup all-purpose flour
1 teaspoon salt
¼ teaspoon pepper
1 cup chicken broth*
1 cup red Burgundy
1 teaspoon garlic salt
1 teaspoon bouquet garni or
    ¼ teaspoon each thyme, basil,
    marjoram and sage
1 jar (2½ ounces) sliced mushrooms
1 can (8¾ ounces) small onions
1 can (16 ounces) whole tiny carrots

Wash chicken and pat dry. In Dutch oven, fry bacon until crisp; drain. Measure flour, salt and pepper into plastic or paper bag. Shake 2 or 3 chicken pieces at a time until all are thoroughly coated. Brown chicken in hot bacon drippings. Drain fat from Dutch oven. Crumble bacon over chicken.

Stir in chicken broth, wine, garlic salt and bouquet garni. Cover; simmer 30 minutes or until thickest pieces are tender. Add mushrooms (with liquid), onions (with liquid) and carrots (with liquid). Cover and simmer 15 minutes longer or until vegetables are heated through. Sprinkle with parsley if desired.

4 servings.

° Chicken broth can be made by dissolving 1 chicken bouillon cube in 1 cup boiling water, or use canned chicken broth.

Clusters of strawflowers make gay party favors. Place them in small wire baskets to accent each place setting.

TIMETABLE

Night before or in the morning:
  Prepare Coq au Vin but do not add vegetables; refrigerate
  Prepare salad ingredients
  Prepare dessert
30 minutes before serving:
  Add vegetables to Coq au Vin; heat through
  Arrange cheese and crackers; serve when guests arrive
20 minutes before:
  Heat rolls
  Make coffee
  Toss salad

SALAD PROVENCE

½ **medium head lettuce, washed and chilled**
1 **small bunch romaine, washed and chilled**
½ **cup cauliflowerets**
⅓ **cup halved pimiento-stuffed olives**
⅓ **cup bottled garlic salad dressing**

Tear greens into bite-size pieces (about 6 cups). Place greens in plastic bag. Add cauliflowerets and olives and refrigerate.

Just before serving, pour salad dressing into bag. Close bag and shake until vegetables and olives are well coated.

4 servings.

FRENCH ROLLS

Heat 1 package (9 ounces) brown and serve French rolls as directed on package. To serve, cut each roll into thirds.

4 servings.

GRAPES AND PINEAPPLE IN SOUR CREAM

2 **cups fresh seedless green grapes or 2 cans (8 ounces each) seedless grapes, drained**
1 **can (13¼ ounces) pineapple chunks, drained**
¼ **cup brown sugar (packed)**
⅓ **cup dairy sour cream**

Combine grapes and pineapple. Reserve 1 tablespoon of the brown sugar; blend remaining sugar and the sour cream. Toss with fruits and chill.

Just before serving, sprinkle with reserved brown sugar.

4 servings.

VARIATION
■ *Strawberries in Sour Cream:* Substitute 3 cups fresh strawberry halves (about 1 pint) for the grapes and pineapple.

STRAWBERRIES TO DIP

Wash 1 pint fresh strawberries; do not hull. Chill. To serve, divide berries among dessert dishes. Pass bowls of sour cream and brown sugar. Guests spoon some of each onto dessert plates and dip berries into the sour cream, then into the sugar.

4 servings.

The host moves onto center stage, flaming the sauce and doing the serving.

*Crystal
and
Candlelight*

Cucumber Spears with Crab Dip
Fruited Rock Cornish Hens
Barley-Mushroom Pilaf
Buttered Broccoli Spears
Garden Salad with Croutons
Pots de Crème

CUCUMBER SPEARS WITH CRAB DIP

1 medium green pepper
1 cup dairy sour cream
1 can (7½ ounces) crabmeat, drained
   and cartilage removed
½ teaspoon garlic salt
¼ teaspoon grated lemon peel
1 large cucumber

Cut thin slice from stem end of pepper. Remove seeds and membranes.

Place sour cream, crabmeat, garlic salt and lemon peel in blender. Blend on medium-high speed until smooth, about 45 seconds, stopping blender twice to scrape sides. Pour into green pepper shell.

Pare cucumber; cut lengthwise into quarters. Remove seeds and cut cucumber quarters into spears, about 2x¾ inch.

4 servings.

Note: Dip can also be served with crackers or crisp vegetables such as radishes or celery, carrot or zucchini sticks.

FRUITED ROCK CORNISH HENS

4 Rock Cornish hens (about 1 pound each)
1 tablespoon onion salt
¼ teaspoon pepper
½ cup butter or margarine, melted
2 tablespoons lemon juice or vinegar
1 tablespoon cornstarch
⅛ teaspoon salt
1 can (11 ounces) mandarin orange
   segments, drained (reserve syrup)
1 jar (8 ounces) maraschino cherries,
   drained (reserve syrup)
2 tablespoons rum or brandy, if desired

Thaw hens if frozen. Heat oven to 400°. Wash hens and pat dry. Mix onion salt and pepper; rub cavities of hens with seasonings. Place hens breast side up on rack in open shallow roasting pan. Brush each with butter. Roast 45 to 60 minutes, basting hens with butter occasionally.

Blend lemon juice, cornstarch and salt in small saucepan. Add water to reserved syrups to measure 1 cup; stir into cornstarch mixture. Cook, stirring constantly, until mixture thickens and boils. Boil and stir 1 minute. Stir fruits into sauce; heat through. To flame, pour fruit sauce into chafing dish over heat. Warm rum; pour over sauce and ignite. Serve sauce with hens.

4 servings.

VARIATION
■ *Bing Cherry Hens:* Substitute 1 can (8¾ ounces) pitted dark sweet cherries for the maraschino cherries.

115

BARLEY-MUSHROOM PILAF

2 tablespoons butter or margarine
1 cup barley
1 can (8 ounces) mushroom stems and pieces, drained (reserve liquid)
3 tablespoons onion flakes
2 teaspoons instant chicken bouillon
1 teaspoon celery salt
⅛ teaspoon pepper

Heat oven to 400°. Melt butter in skillet. Cook and stir barley and mushrooms in butter 1 minute. Place in ungreased 1½-quart casserole. Add boiling water to reserved liquid to measure 3 cups; pour over barley and mushrooms. Stir in remaining ingredients. Cover; bake 50 to 60 minutes, stirring once after 30 minutes.

4 to 6 servings.

TIMETABLE

Night before or in the morning:
Thaw hens if frozen
Prepare dessert
Prepare appetizer; refrigerate
Prepare salad greens; refrigerate

1 hour 15 minutes before serving:
Prepare and bake pilaf
Prepare and roast hens

20 minutes before:
Cook 2 packages (10 ounces each) frozen broccoli spears
Make sauce for hens
Toss and garnish salad

GARDEN SALAD WITH CROUTONS

1 head Boston lettuce, washed and chilled
1 bunch leaf lettuce, washed and chilled
⅓ cup bottled Italian salad dressing
Croutons
Grated Parmesan cheese

Into bowl, tear greens into bite-size pieces (about 6 cups). Pour dressing over greens; toss until leaves glisten. Sprinkle with croutons and cheese.

4 servings.

POTS DE CRÈME

1 bar (4 ounces) sweet cooking chocolate
2 tablespoons sugar
¾ cup light cream
2 egg yolks, slightly beaten
½ teaspoon vanilla

Heat chocolate, sugar and cream over medium heat, stirring constantly, until chocolate is melted and mixture is smooth. Remove from heat; gradually beat into egg yolks. Blend in vanilla. Pour into pots de crème cups, demitasse cups or other small serving dishes. Chill. If desired, garnish with whipped cream or frozen whipped topping.

4 servings.

Party Pointers

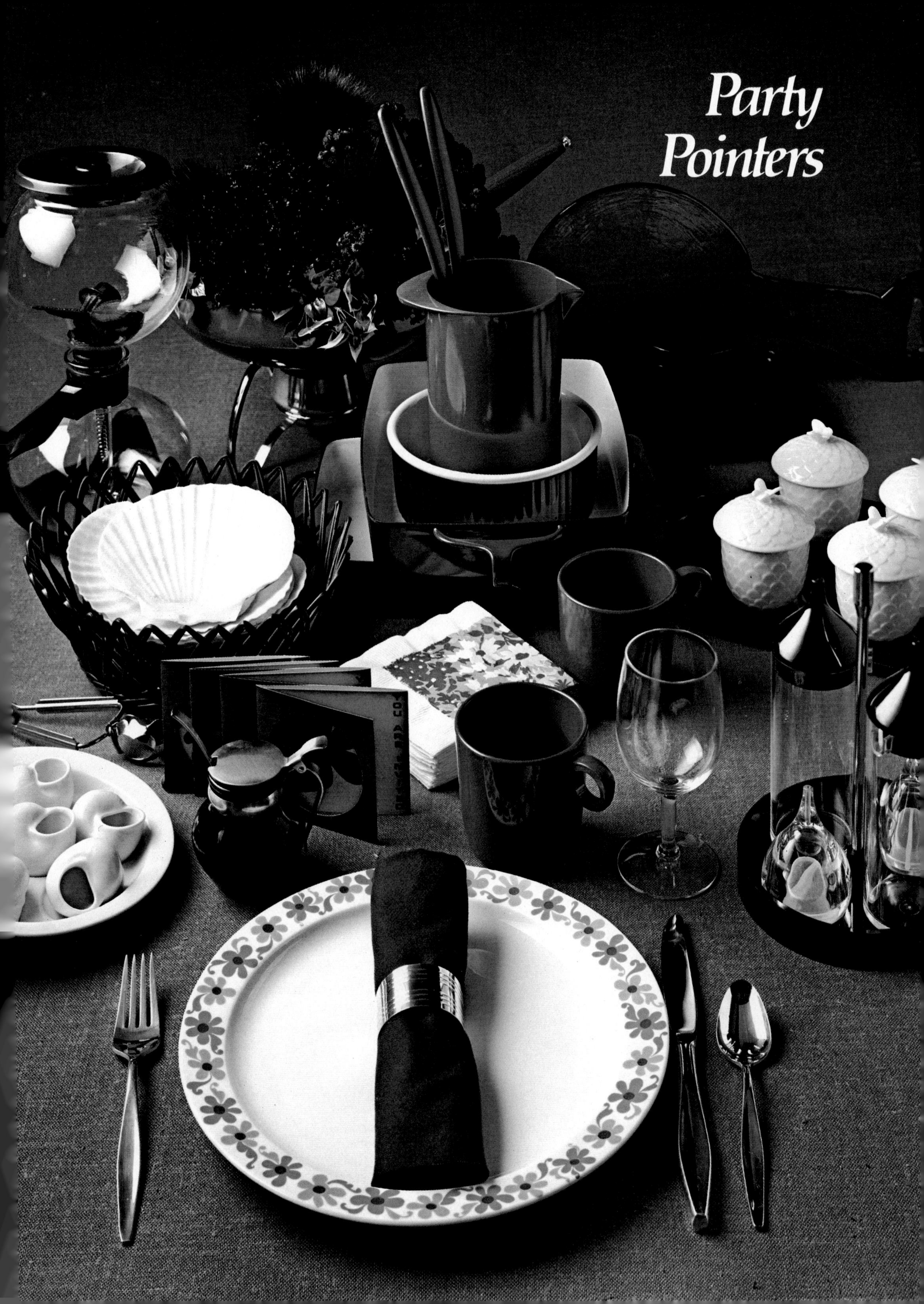

Party Pointers

Entertaining! Like the old gray mare, it's not what it used to be. When our grandmothers, or even our mothers, gave parties, the table was set with service plates, finger bowls and three kinds of fork. This is pretty much a thing of the past. So are the four- and five-course menus that a dinner party used to call for.

Today, more women work, people live in smaller houses and apartments, more attention is paid to diet. Add these factors to an ever-proliferating choice of convenience foods from supermarket and delicatessen. Result? Dinner parties have become less formal, more varied as to service and infinitely easier on the hostess-cook.

The first step toward ensuring a successful dinner party is taking honest stock of your resources. How big is your kitchen? If it's postage-stamp size, think about something that cooks in one big pot, pan or casserole. Or consider doing some of the cooking at the table or on the outdoor grill.

How many people can be comfortably seated at your dining table? If the space is limited, look around for another spot to serve the meal—the living room, family room, porch or terrace are all relaxed settings, in key with today's easy informality.

What about your supply of china, silver and glassware? If it's inadequate for the guest list you have in mind, mix patterns. Or buy inexpensive plates in bright colors and ask a friend to lend you flatware.

And most important—how practiced a cook are you? If you're new at the game, don't let that deter you. Just choose something easy—we have dozens of suggestions for you in this book. And be sure you try it out once or twice before presenting it to guests.

Even spur-of-the-moment parties are based on foresight. The kind of foresight that stocks a good selection of foods in the freezer and on the kitchen shelves. Then all you need is a little prior practice in putting them together so that a guestworthy spread can be assembled quickly and attractively.

We've grouped our menus into four types of parties: casual and impromptu dinners, just what they imply, and possibly the most "now" entertaining there is; cook-at-the-table menus that make things easy on the hostess and fun for guests; buffets, to be served and eaten anywhere; and sit-down dinners, updated but still gracious.

This chapter supplements the recipes, menus, timetables and specific party information contained in the book. Here you'll find general information relating to giving dinner parties. Things like preparation hints, equipment to have, garnishes and ideas for setting a pretty table. In short, the myriad details that combine to create the festive mood that makes your dinner a party.

118

GETTING THE HOUSE PARTY-READY

Obviously the more work you do in advance, the less you'll have to think about when the guests arrive. And you can relax and enjoy your own party from beginning to end.

Make the following preparations several days before the party:

☐ Get any major cleaning out of the way early.

☐ Check linens, dinnerware, flatware and accessories; then do any washing, polishing or augmenting necessary.

☐ Take inventory of the equipment and utensils the recipes call for.

☐ Shop for all foods except perishables.

☐ Freeze a good supply of ice cubes (plastic bags are good for storage).

Then the night before the party you can:

☐ Do last-minute cleaning, put out guest towels, check space and hangers in the guest closet.

☐ Set the table. (Cover it with a cloth or piece of plastic if you like.)

☐ Arrange centerpiece and other decorations.

TABLE TOPPERS

Color—it sets a party mood immediately. A table covering that contributes color and contrast to your china and serving pieces is a great attention-getter.

Place mats, runners or a versatile tablecloth are in keeping with today's casual entertaining. All of these come in a wide variety of fabrics, colors and patterns. Thus the hostess has a chance to play artist.

For example: Mix a solid color cloth with patterned napkins. Or use runners along both sides of the table.

Whatever you use to cover your table should reflect your taste and please you. If it does, it's bound to be a success!

SIT-DOWN DINNERS

The First Course: Often it's easier to serve your starter in the living room. It's always a good idea to keep it light and simple—raw vegetable sticks with a dip, glasses of fruit punch or mugs of hot or cold bouillon. Plan on something that will sharpen the appetite, not dull it.

The Table Setting: In the dining room the table has been set for the course or courses that will follow. The silver is placed one inch from the edge of the table and arranged so that the pieces to be used first are on the outside. Forks go to the left of the plate, knives (with blades turned inward) and spoons to the right.

Three exceptions: Seafood forks (if you're using them) are usually placed on the right, beyond the spoons; the butter knife is placed vertically or horizontally on the butter plate (which is above the dinner fork); the fork can be placed on the right when no other flatware is needed.

If a salad is being served as part of the main course, the salad plate should be at the left of the forks with the salad fork either to the right or left of the dinner fork. Dessert silver may be included in the original setting or brought in with the dessert.

Glasses are placed above the knife, with wine glasses to the right of the water glasses. When tea or coffee accompanies the meal, the cup and saucer go slightly above and to the right of the spoons. The napkin may be placed on the plate or to the left of the forks.

BUFFETS

The Locale: Flexibility is the operative word here, since a buffet can be served anywhere. The dining table itself can be the buffet table, but you might also use the coffee table, a desk, low book cases, the kitchen counter, a room divider or even an ironing board covered with a gay fabric.

The Decor: Wherever you're serving, cover the buffet "table" with a bright cloth or runner. If space allows, have a festive centerpiece of flowers, greens, gourds or candles. Or use an interesting item from your home—maybe a painting or sculpture. If there isn't room for extras, make your most dramatic dish the focal point.

If the dinner is to be eaten at card tables these too can be made festive—decorations here should be small-scale. One inexpensive but conversation-making idea is to cut place mats from heavy patterned gift wrapping paper. Motifs from the wrapping paper can then be cut out and glued on color-coordinated paper napkins.

The Traffic Pattern: For a large crowd, you may want to have two serving lines, with double orders of everything duplicating each other along both sides of the table. But one line or two, the order should be the same. Plates first, main course and vegetables next, then salad, condiments, rolls, and finally silver and napkins. Each dish should be easily reached and accompanied by good-sized serving pieces.

Dessert Service: While guests are finishing seconds of the main course, the hostess clears the buffet and arranges dessert, dessert plates and silver. Coffee can be served with dessert or both can be served later, in the living room.

SPECIAL PARTY EQUIPMENT

Besides your standard cooking utensils there are certain pieces of equipment that make a party party-er, add a flourish to the cooking and serving of special dishes or hold food handsomely at a just-right temperature.

Unless you're a full-time gourmet cook, the chances are you won't need or want all the items listed below, but a few of them *will* make your entertaining easier—and perhaps encourage you to master some exciting new dishes. Incidentally, there's no law against friends and neighbors pooling their resources. So why not lend your own prize pieces for other people's parties and borrow what you don't have for your own?

Automatic coffee maker
Bundt pan
Butane gas burner
Candle warmer
Carving set
Chafing dish
Cook-and-serve equipment
Crêpe or omelet pan
Electric bun warmer
Electric knife
Electric skillet
Electric warming tray
Espresso coffee maker
Fondue set
Gelatin molds
Paella pan
Portable broiler and/or oven
Pots de crème
Serving cart
Snail sets
Soufflé dishes
Trays
TV tables
Wok pan

TABLE-COOKING EQUIPMENT

Naturally if it's going to appear on the dinner table, you'll want your cooking equipment to be attractive. Bear in mind that the cook-and-serve dishes made today are bright additions as well as practical. Keep your recipe in mind, too—it's important to know which utensil does which job best.

Chafing dishes are very versatile. Almost any food that can be prepared in a saucepan or skillet can be made in a chafing dish—if the heat is suitably adjusted. However, because top-of-the-range cooking usually takes considerably less time, many people cook the food in the kitchen and use a chafing dish for at-table serving and to keep the food warm.

Flameproof earthenware pots are decorative additions to your table—they are excellent for cheese fondues.

Metal fondue pots with an inward curve at the top are recommended for beef fondues. The metal allows the high temperature necessary and the curve is a safeguard against spatter.

All-purpose pots are extremely practical. If you want to make one utensil serve all purposes, choose a porcelainized cast-iron pot; it can be heated moderately for cheese and very hot for oil.

Electric skillets, fondue pots or saucepans are also popular for table-top cooking; the heat can be easily regulated.

Sources of heat can be canned fuel, an alcohol burner using denatured alcohol, a butane gas burner, electric heating unit or candle warmer. Be sure to read instructions carefully for each type and plan your cooking accordingly (some of these heats are fine for keeping food warm, but not for actual cooking). Never refill an alcohol burner while hot. Keep all sources of heat out of direct drafts.

PLAYING THE ACCESSORIES GAME

One mark of a good hostess is inventiveness—the ability to make do ingeniously with what she has. If you want to serve something and don't have the conventional dishes for serving it, use your imagination. Something you do have may be even more attractive.

When your party is still in the planning stage, take inventory of the accessory pieces on your shelves; you'll probably discover that virtually every one of them can do double, triple or quadruple duty. For example, use:

☐ *Large salad bowls* for fruit, rolls, snacks, cookies or as a centerpiece container for almost anything you like.
☐ *Small salad bowls* for nuts, snacks, sauces, candy.
☐ *Soup tureens* for chili, stew, spaghetti.
☐ *Large brandy snifters* for tossed salad, popcorn, cookies, fresh or frozen fruits, colorful combinations of sherbet or ice-cream balls.
☐ *Footed cake plates* for appetizers, arrangements of individual desserts, little bowls of curry go-alongs.
☐ *Ice buckets* for tossed salad, snacks, popcorn, cookies, fruit.
☐ *Fondue pots* for soup, chili, stew, hot punch, hot dips, warm dessert sauces.
☐ *Coffee mugs* for soup, raw vegetable sticks, pretzel sticks, ice cream.
☐ *Chafing dishes* for hors d'oeuvres, crêpes, warm dessert sauces.
☐ *Baking shells* for seafood dishes, salads, bread-and-butter plates.

121

MAIN DISH GARNISHES

The little extras you add to a meat platter to make it more attractive should be colorful and appetizing. And they can also be an integral part of the menu. So although you arrange them at the last minute, they should be planned ahead with the rest of the meal.

Consider other foods in the meal for possible garnishes (serving the vegetable on the same platter is often a good idea). In general, a fruit or vegetable that complements the meat's flavor is a pretty and tasty choice. With turkey or chicken, for example, you may want to serve cranberry relish or mashed yams in orange cups or hot peach halves filled with chutney or pickle relish.

With beef, try broiled tomato halves or sautéed cherry tomatoes with parsley or use oven-browned potatoes and/or mushroom caps to ring the platter.

Pork takes kindly to spiced apple rings with apple-mint jelly in the center, while ham is particularly handsome surrounded by pineapple slices topped with spiced crab apples.

When you're serving fish, make lemon twists and tuck parsley around them.

With lamb you might fill pears with mint jelly or bed spiced apricots on mint leaves.

Casseroles can be enhanced with parsley, watercress, pimiento strips, green pepper rings, olives or slivered nuts. Actually many of these garnishing ideas are applicable to several types of meat. Just be sure they're bright and fresh looking, and as hot or cold as they should be.

DINING WITH WINE

Some people feel that all it takes to make any meal a party is a bottle of wine. And more and more young hostesses are discovering the pleasures of wine. In the past the rule has been that red wine was served with red meat and white wine with poultry and fish. But today it's customary to serve whatever you like best, regardless of color. There are still a few guidelines, though. If the food is rich, the wine should be full flavored. Similarly, a delicate meal calls for a light wine. Some foods, such as curries and highly spiced dishes, should not have wines served with them; the strongly seasoned flavor kills the taste of the wine. Beer is an ideal accompaniment for spicy food.

Wines served with a meal should usually be dry; sweeter wines are for dessert only. Red wines and dessert wines should be served at a cool room temperature; white and rosé wines should be well chilled.

Here we give you some traditional combinations—but don't feel bound by them. Wine is meant to be an enjoyable accompaniment to a meal, so you should serve whatever pleases you.

With roasts, steaks, stews or game—Burgundy, claret or rosé. With poultry, fish or cheese dishes—Chablis, Rhine wine or Sauterne. With anything, any time—a sparkling wine such as champagne.

As for glasses, one set can serve for all purposes. Choose clear 9-ounce glasses with bowls that curve gracefully inward. Fill the glass only about half full so the bouquet can expand—the aroma of wine is part of its pleasure.

Wine pouring is considered a male prerogative, so let your husband do the honors. If you are entertaining without a host, ask one of your male guests to play sommelier.

ALWAYS ON HAND

Terrific party insurance—a well-stocked freezer and a cupboard filled with the delicious things that come in packages, cans and jars. With this kind of money-in-the-bank, you're ready to entertain on short notice just about anytime.

Home-cooked foods you can prepare in advance and freeze:

Breads
Cakes
Casseroles
Cookies
Cream puffs (page 103)
Cut-up cooked turkey or chicken
Dinner rolls
Pie shells
Pies (except custard, cream or meringue-topped)
Popovers

Convenience foods to store in the freezer:

Cake or cookies
Fish, shrimp and other seafood
Fruits and vegetables
Ice cream or sherbet
Soups
Turkey roast

Convenience foods for the cupboard:

PACKAGED

Buttermilk baking mix
Casserole mixes (scalloped and au gratin potatoes, rice and noodle mixes)
Dessert mixes
Dry bread crumbs
Grated Parmesan cheese
Herbed croutons
Instant mashed potato puffs
Instant rice
Soup, gravy and salad dressing mixes
Spaghetti, macaroni, noodles

CANNED

Bottled salad dressings
Ham, tuna, salmon, shrimp, crabmeat, chipped beef, corned beef, luncheon meats
Mushrooms
Pickles, olives, relishes
Pimiento
Ready-to-serve puddings and sauces
Soups (bouillon, chicken, consommé, mushroom, tomato)

FOR THE SPICE RACK

Herbs and spices can add a highlight of flavor to soups, vegetables, casseroles, stews, salad dressings and sauces. Be sure to have all, or at least your favorites among the following, on hand.

Allspice
Basil
Bay leaves
Celery seed
Chili powder
Cinnamon
Cloves
Curry powder
Dill seed and weed
Garlic salt
Ginger
Instant minced onion
Mace
Marjoram
Mustard
Nutmeg
Onion salt
Oregano
Paprika
Parsley flakes
Sage
Savory
Seasoned salt
Thyme

Index